THE
HERO
INSIDE OF YOU

*260 Thrilling and Inspiring True Stories
of Ordinary Heroes*

ALLAN ZULLO AND **MARA BOVSUN**

SOURCEBOOKS, INC.
NAPERVILLE, ILLINOIS

Published by Sourcebooks, Inc.
P.O. Box 4410, Naperville, Illinois 60567-4410
(630) 961-3900
Fax: (630) 961-2168
www.sourcebooks.com

Library of Congress Cataloging-in-Publication Data

Zullo, Allan.
  The hero inside of you : 260 thrilling and inspiring true stories of ordinary heroes / Allan Zullo and Mara Bovsun.
     p. cm.
  ISBN-13: 978-1-4022-0717-4
  ISBN-10: 1-4022-0717-4
 1. Heroes--Biography. 2. Courage. 3. Inspiration. I. Bovsun, Mara. II. Title.

CT105.Z65 2006
920.02--dc22

2006020832

Printed and bound in the United States of America
CH 10 9 8 7 6 5 4 3 2 1

To Roseville, Illinois' finest—Frank Lang, Vic Twomey,
Bill Berg, Dan Patch, John Hill, Leonard Arnold
and Tink Hoyt—who served their country with
honor and bravery.

INTRODUCTION

In these turbulent times, we need heroes more than ever. Luckily, there are heroes all around us—and not just on the silver screen or in the sports arena. *The Hero Inside of You* features stories of extraordinary men, women, and children—and even pets—who went far beyond the call of duty to help others. For example, the one-legged man who dashed through flames to save an old woman, the schoolteacher who thwarted a crazed gunman, the grandma who leapt on a crocodile to save a man from the jaws of death, the coed who gave up a cushy life in America to help children in India's slums, and the dog that became a hero during the sinking of the *Titanic*. This book celebrates the heroes among us—those courageous souls who did the right thing no matter what the risk.

*"Heroes embrace life;
the world expands and becomes
less menacing and more hopeful
by their very existence."*

—Noel Annan, English educator and historian

HIKER TURNS HERO IN KILLER AVALANCHE

Kenneth Rutland was hiking on a challenging trail on Grouse Mountain in North Vancouver, British Columbia, in 1999 when he heard a rumbling that turned into a deafening roar. It was the unmistakable sound of an avalanche. He watched in horror as a wall of snow swept away five hikers. When the slide subsided, Rutland, thirty-eight, heard muffled moans under the snow and started digging with his bare hands. He freed two injured hikers when another avalanche struck. Rutland held tight to one of the hikers and rode the white wave blindly down the mountain until they ended up buried under heavy snow. Exhausted, Rutland dug through the icy prison to free himself before pulling out the two hikers. For his bravery, Rutland was awarded Canada's Star of Courage.

You can read more about the avalanche in *Star of Courage* by John Melady (Dundurn Press).

BRAKES FAIL, BUT NOT TRUCKER'S BRAVERY

When his brakes failed, trucker Bryan Decker, twenty-six, hurtled helplessly down a mountain road near San Jose, California, in his 18-wheeler loaded with twenty-five tons of sand. Up ahead was a traffic jam. Decker had a split second to make a grave decision: plow into the cars ahead of him and kill many people or steer his truck off a three-hundred-foot cliff, losing only one life—his own. For Decker, there was no choice. He turned the truck toward the cliff, telling himself, *Better that just one dies than those people in front of me.* As his truck crashed through the brush and bounced off boulders, he thought, *This is it, pal. You're a goner.* Just a few feet before it reached the edge of the cliff, the cab slammed into a tree and came to a rest. Decker emerged from his ordeal, which happened in 1981, with hip and back injuries and a gash on his forehead. The courageous trucker said it was a small price to pay for preventing an untold number of deaths.

DOCTOR'S DANGEROUS GAMBLE PAYS OFF

His peers laughed and said he was dead wrong, even nuts, but Australian physician Barry Marshall would not back down. For years, the medical establishment said that stomach ulcers were the result of excess acid. Dr. Marshall was certain there was another cause—a bacterium known as *Helicobacter pylori*, which could be cured quickly and inexpensively with antibiotics. His colleagues scoffed at him. So in 1984 a frustrated Dr. Marshall decided to prove his point—using his own body. He swallowed a cocktail containing a toxic dose of *H. pylori*. He became very sick, and after two weeks his stomach showed signs of ulcers. He treated them with antibiotics and was soon cured. His experiment jolted the scientific community and led to research that changed the way doctors treat this serious condition.

WOMAN SAVED FROM FLAMING CAR

On a wintry January day in 2002 near Knoxville, Maryland, Nancy Hay, forty-six, lost control of her car on an icy highway and slammed into a guardrail, rupturing the fuel tank. As flames swirled around the car, Hay was unable to escape. Salesman Jason Paul Gordon, twenty-seven, who witnessed the accident, raced toward the burning car, but he couldn't get through the flames to open the driver's door. He tried to break the windshield with his fists, but had no luck. Just then another passerby tossed Gordon a snow shovel, which he used to smash the windshield, creating a hole big enough to pull Hay from the car seconds before the interior burst into flames. Thanks to Gordon's quick actions, Hay sustained only minor injuries.

HOMELESS OLD DOG
SAVES LOST BOY

When her owner died in 1972, Brandy, a golden retriever, ended up on the street, surviving on scraps of food left by people in Middletown, New York. Weeks later, Sara Whalen's eighteen-month-old son, Adam, wandered off, triggering a massive search. Just when it seemed futile, searchers heard frantic barking and followed the sound, which led them to Adam, who was leaning against a tree, asleep. In front of him was Brandy, straining hard to prop him up—just inches from a thirty-five-foot drop to a stream below. Authorities later said that had Brandy not been there pinning Adam to the tree, he most likely would have fallen and died. Sara was so thankful, she adopted the dog and started a sanctuary, Pets Alive, which is devoted to saving homeless animals.

For more information: www.petsalive.com

ONE-MAN SWAT TEAM
BATTLES WASPS

In 2002, the people of Pawarenga, New Zealand, were harassed by angry wasps that lived in a car-sized nest atop an eighty-three-foot tree. When the government refused to help, a local man, Mike Knight, volunteered to get rid of the nasty insects. Wearing a wetsuit and a bee-keeper's mask for protection, Knight was tethered to a helicopter that hovered over the nest. He was lowered on a rope until he was able to poke a hole in the top of the nest and pour canisters of insecticide inside. Thousands of fighting-mad wasps swarmed out and attacked him, covering his entire body as the helicopter whisked him away. He was lowered to a field where helpers doused him with insecticide, killing the wasps. Crazy as it seems, Knight's heroic efforts worked. Wasps were no longer a problem in Pawarenga. Amazingly, Knight claimed he didn't suffer a single sting.

ROPE EXPERT RESCUES BRIDGE JUMPER

Andrew Vince, thirty-four, a rappelling instructor, was giving a demonstration of his craft at a charity event on the ninety-foot-high Tyne Bridge in Northumbria, England, in January 2004 when he heard people yelling that a suicidal woman was hanging over the side at the other end of the bridge. Vince raced over to help. When he arrived, two policemen were on their stomachs desperately trying to hold on to a nineteen-year-old woman who was dangling over the side, but they were losing their grip. Vince swiftly secured his rope to the bridge, jumped over the side, swooped down, and grabbed the woman with one arm. He then brought her back up onto the bridge. "I was in the right place at the right time with the right equipment," he said.

COED NEARLY DIES AFTER SOUNDING ALARM

When fire bells rang out in a dorm in New Jersey's Seton Hall University on a January night in 2000, many students stayed in bed, figuring it was just another false alarm. But senior Dana Christmas, the dorm's resident assistant, smelled smoke. "It's a real fire this time!" she yelled as she ran down the halls, banging on doors. Rather than flee, Dana kept alerting her fellow students until she collapsed from the thickening smoke. Just before losing consciousness in the worsening fire, she thought, *It's time for me to go to heaven.* Minutes later, firefighters rescued Dana, who remained in a coma for months and suffered burns over 60 percent of her body. Fortunately, she recovered, and doesn't regret risking her life. "How could I leave them?" she said later. The fire, which authorities believe was arson, killed three and injured fifty-eight, but the toll would have been higher without Dana's heroism.

For information on the Dana Christmas Scholarship for Heroism: www.hesaa.org/students/aid_programs

MAN DEVOTES LIFE TO SPRINGING THE WRONGLY ACCUSED

By his mid-thirties, Jim McCloskey was a wealthy businessman who decided his life was "shallow, selfish, superficial, and inauthentic" and chucked it all to become a Presbyterian minister. As part of his training, he was assigned to Trenton's New Jersey State Prison. There, in 1980, he met convicted murderer Jorge "Chiefie" De Los Santos, who swore he didn't do it. McCloskey believed him. Running through much of his life savings, McCloskey finally found the real killer and got him to confess. De Los Santos was set free, spurring McCloskey to create the Centurion Ministries, a group devoted to proving the innocence of the wrongly accused. To date he has helped more than two dozen prisoners.

For more information: www.centurionministries.org

BYSTANDER SAVES DROWNING PLANE CRASH SURVIVOR

In 1982, an Air Florida jet departing from Washington, D.C., crashed into the Potomac River, dumping flaming debris, bodies, and a handful of survivors into the freezing river. One survivor, Patricia Tirado, twenty-three, was floundering in the water and couldn't summon the strength to hold onto the lifeline that had been lowered by a rescue helicopter. Watching the drama unfold from the riverbank, Lenny Skutnik, twenty-eight, a government clerk, couldn't stand by and let her die. He ripped off his coat, plunged into the frigid water, swam to Tirado, and pulled her safely to shore. "I knew she wasn't going to make it, so I dove in," he explained later. Skutnik's brave act earned him a seat next to First Lady Nancy Reagan at the State of the Union Address, where President Ronald Reagan publicly thanked him for his heroism.

"*Courage is being scared to death...
and saddling up anyway.*"

—John Wayne, actor

HERO FROM HISTORY
Dr. Martin Luther King Jr.

D r. Martin Luther King Jr. gave his life for a dream. "I have a dream that my four children will one day live in a nation where they will not be judged by the color of their skin but by the content of their character," he said in one of America's most stirring speeches. King was the leading light of the civil rights movement during its greatest achievements in the 1960s. When other activists beat the drums of violence, Dr. King preached peaceful resistance. Arrested, stabbed, threatened, and jeered, King never backed off in his crusade for equality. In 1964, at thirty-six, he became the youngest Nobel Peace Prize laureate. Four years later an assassin's bullet cut him down, but his message lives on. "Let us not seek to satisfy our thirst for freedom by drinking from the cup of bitterness and hatred," he said. "We must forever conduct our struggle on the high plane of dignity and discipline."

For more information: www.stanford.edu/group/King

SOLDIER THROWS HIMSELF ON GRENADE TO SAVE COMRADES

Leslie Bellrichard, a twenty-year-old private from Janesville, Wisconsin, was one of three hundred American soldiers defending a hilltop that was under attack by the Vietcong. During the fierce 1967 firefight, a grenade landed near Bellrichard. Knowing he didn't have time to run over, pick it up, and throw it back, he selflessly fell on the grenade. A split second later it exploded, killing him instantly. His heroic action saved several of his fellow soldiers from death or serious injuries. Bellrichard was among sixteen men killed and sixty-three wounded on the hill that night. For sacrificing his life to save others, Bellrichard was one of two soldiers to posthumously receive the Medal of Honor from that horrific battle. The other soldier was Sergeant Frankie Molnar, who also died after throwing himself onto a grenade.

For more information about Medals of Honor:
www.cmohs.org

DEADLY CROC NO MATCH FOR PLUCKY GRANDMA

Alicia Sorohan, a sixty-year-old grandmother, was asleep at her beach campsite in Bathhurst Bay, Australia, early one morning in 2004 when she heard bloodcurdling screams. She rushed out of her tent and saw that a fourteen-foot crocodile had grabbed nearby camper Andrew Kerr, thirty-four, by the legs and was dragging him out of his tent. Sorohan leapt onto the head of the croc and beat it until it let Kerr go and attacked her. But then Sorohan's son Jason, thirty-five, shot and killed the reptile. "I just did what I had to do," said the modest crocodile wrestler, who broke her nose, cracked several teeth, and nearly lost an arm in the struggle. "I'm no hero." But Kerr disagreed. "It was like seeing an angel," he said of Sorohan's fight with the croc. Local newspapers began calling her "Crocodile Gran-Dee."

BEACHGOER FIGHTS UNDERTOW TO RESCUE DROWNING GIRLS

While wading in the waters at Florida's Panama City Beach in 2002, Jennifer Jackson and Hayden Strickland, both fourteen, suddenly became trapped by a powerful undertow. Seeing the girls in trouble, beachgoer Jared Williams, sixteen, dove into the water to save them. Struggling in the treacherous surf, Jared first reached Hayden and dragged her to shore before diving back in for Jennifer, who was nearly exhausted. He grabbed her, then swam parallel to the beach before making a beeline for the shore. A woman with a bodyboard waded out to meet them and helped Jennifer from the water. Both girls recovered, thanks to Jared's lifesaving actions.

AMERICAN TEEN BRINGS HOPE TO INDIA'S SLUMS

Shaheen Mistri was a typical college-bound American teenager when she visited Mumbai, India, on a holiday in 1990. Instead of hitting the tourist spots, Mistri visited the slums and fell in love with the children there. When her vacation ended, she stayed on, determined to help them. The following year Mistri established her first center in Mumbai—a school for fifteen underprivileged children—and called it Akanksha, which means "hope" in Hindi. "I decided we'd just start and learn along the way," she said. Relying on volunteers and donations, the Akanksha Foundation has blossomed to thirty-six centers, which have served more than sixteen hundred children from the slums.

For more information: www.akanksha.org

"*Courage is not the absence of fear,
but rather the judgment that
something else is more important
than fear.*"

—Ambrose Redmoon, paraplegic writer

TEACHER CAPTURES
MASS MURDERER

Art and history teacher Rainer Heise, sixty, was supervising a painting class at a grammar school in Erfurt, Germany, in 2002 when he heard shots and screams. He slipped out of his classroom and caught a glimpse of a gunman dressed in black from head to toe. When the shooting continued, Heise bravely confronted the assailant, who ripped off his black mask. Heise recognized him as former pupil Robert Steinhauser, nineteen, a troublemaker who had been expelled a year earlier. Heise challenged him, "If you plan to shoot me, then look in my eyes." The gunman lowered his pistol and said, "I've done enough for one day, Mr. Heise." Steinhauser had murdered seventeen teachers and students. Heise took the gun and locked Steinhauser in a closet. The teacher didn't know that Steinhauser had another gun—one he used on himself. Heise was hailed as a hero. "Who knows how many more would've been killed if he hadn't confronted the gunman," said a policeman.

PLUMBER SAVES WORKER FROM SUFFOCATING

A combination of thin air and gas fumes caused construction worker Jon Stanger, thirty-five, to pass out while repairing an underground sump, or pit, above a buried gasoline storage tank at a convenience store in Escondido, California, in 2003. Smelling the fumes, Richard Moten, a fifty-year-old plumber, knew that Stanger would suffocate within minutes, so he jumped six feet down into the poisonous sump. Holding his breath, Moten picked up the unconscious man, put him over his shoulder, and struggled to get out. His lungs ready to burst, Moten found a foothold about two feet up. From there, he was able to hoist Stanger to people waiting above who pulled both from the deadly sump. "The emergency room doctor told me that if [Moten] hadn't been there, I'd be planning a funeral," Stanger's wife, Kerrie, said after he recovered. Moten replied, "You just do what you have to do."

BOY RUN OVER WHILE SHOVING PAL FROM TRUCK'S PATH

As best friends Jay Corrie, nine, and Jack Briggs, five, were crossing a street near their homes in Houghton-le-Spring, England, in 2003, a seven-ton truck lost control. Jay spotted the vehicle, which was barreling toward Jack. Without hesitation, the older boy shoved his pal out of the way of the oncoming truck, taking the brunt of the impact. Both suffered serious head injuries but police said there was no doubt that Jack would have died without Jay's courageous act. A few months later both had recovered enough to attend a ceremony and reception at 10 Downing Street, where Jay was given an award for bravery.

HARLEM WOMAN GIVES LOVE, HOPE TO DRUG BABIES

In 1969, a poor Harlem woman opened her home and heart to a drug addict's baby. Word spread and within two months, Clara Hale—known simply as Mother Hale—found herself caring for twenty-two babies whose legacy from their parents was a heroin habit. With the help of city officials, Clara established Hale House, where, until her death in 1992, she cared for more than five hundred infants, weaning them from the drug addictions acquired in the womb. "Those babies don't know anything except fear and pain," Mother Hale once said. "It's a hard enough life without coming into it as a second-class citizen. I try to change that."

For more information: www.halehouse.org

BOY'S TUG-OF-WAR WITH WOLF SAVES BROTHER

Helder Barreira, a thirteen-year-old shepherd in Curros, Portugal, was guarding his flock one day in 1979 when a wolf leapt out of the woods and snatched his six-year-old brother, Marcial. The vicious beast had the child by the throat, so Helder knew he had to act fast. In desperation, he grabbed his brother's arm and yanked, engaging the animal in a terrifying life-or-death tug-of-war. Finally, with one great hard pull and a shout, he freed Marcial. Helder then lifted his bleeding brother onto his shoulders and ran, but the wolf chased them. It kept trying to attack again and again, but Helder kept it at bay by hitting it with rocks and sticks, all the while carrying his brother. Near exhaustion, Helder finally forced the wolf to retreat. Helder then staggered out of the forest and lugged his brother to the nearest doctor, who treated him for severe bites.

DOG COMES TO THE RESCUE

While looking for a stranded mare in January 2004, Lisa Parker, of Richmond Dale, Ohio, slipped and fell into a creek. Soaked and freezing, she was having trouble pulling herself out of the icy water and began screaming into the night. Her dog Biyou, an Australian shepherd–wolf cross, was asleep in the barn. But when Biyou heard her owner's cries, the dog ran down to the creek and jumped in. Biyou let Parker grab her heavy fur and then dragged the woman out to safety. Parker is convinced that Biyou knew she was in danger of freezing to death. "That wasn't instinct," Parker told *U.S. News & World Report*. "That was intelligence and courage."

You can read about more heroic dogs in *Dogmania: Amazing but True Canine Stories* by Allan Zullo and Mara Bovsun (Andrews McMeel Publishing, 2006).

IGNORING OWN FEAR OF HEIGHTS, MAN SAVES YOUTH

Parking garage manager Terry Kingsland, fifty-eight, of Stevenage, England, had a paralyzing fear of heights, but that didn't stop him from helping a suicidal teenager in 2004. Kingsland was ending his shift at the Hunter's Bridge Car Park when he learned that a teenage boy was threatening to jump off the fourth-floor parapet. When Kingsland confronted the would-be jumper, the boy said, "I'll be out of your hair in a couple of minutes." Kingsland held out his hand, but when the teen refused to budge, Kingsland inched a little closer out onto the parapet, trying hard to ignore his acrophobia. Kingsland kept talking to the boy, encouraging him to step back. When Kingsland reached out again, the sobbing youth took his hand, allowing Kingsland to guide him off the parapet. "The young lad did much more for me than I did for him," said Kingsland. "I got a buzz out of helping somebody."

PASSERBY RESCUES BURNING WOMAN

Karen Richardson, thirty-five, was driving home one night in 2000 when she spotted thick smoke coming from a house in Lombard, Illinois. Suddenly, she saw an elderly woman standing in the doorway with her clothes on fire. Richardson immediately called 911 on her cell phone, leapt out of her vehicle, and ran to rescue eighty-seven-year-old Hiroko Horino. "I grabbed her by her jacket, and she was on fire," Richardson recalled. "I put her on the ground and rolled her on the grass until the fire was out and picked her up and moved her away from the house for fear it would explode." Thanks to Richardson's quick actions and bravery, Mrs. Horino suffered only minor burns.

DRIVER LETS RUNAWAY RIG RAM HIS TRUCK TO STOP IT

Anthony Borgia saved an untold number of persons from being struck by a runaway tractor-trailer near Scranton, Pennsylvania, in 1978. When he saw that the truck had lost its brakes while on a downgrade toward a busy intersection, Borgia, fifty-five, decided to use the dump truck he was driving to stop the runaway vehicle. He moved into position in front of the rig and let it strike the rear of his dump truck. Although the heavy rig forced the truck into oncoming traffic, Borgia refused to get out of the way. With the two vehicles remaining in contact, they descended the grade without mishap as Borgia carefully applied his brakes. He then moved onto the dirt shoulder of the road, where he stopped the truck and the tractor-trailer about two hundred feet from the intersection.

STORE CLERK SAVES COP IN BANK ROBBER CHASE

Terry Mitchum, a clerk at a shopping center in Lavonia, Georgia, helped subdue a violent bank robber and saved the life of a police officer in 2000. Mitchum saw the bandit leaving the center after robbing the Northeast Georgia bank branch. Recalled Mitchum, "He took off in the car, and I ran next door to the police department." Mitchum got into the police car with Police Chief Randy Shirley and they took off in pursuit, reaching speeds of 110 mph. The robber's car got stuck in a field, so he took off on foot with Chief Shirley close behind. Mitchum then heard gunshots and saw the chief and the crook locked in a desperate struggle. "The man had a grip on Chief Shirley's gun and then the chief started yelling for help," Mitchum said. He grabbed the suspect from behind and pushed him to the ground. The modest clerk was surprised when the Carnegie Hero Fund recognized his courage. "I think anyone would have reacted like I did," he said.

For more information: www.carnegiehero.org

"*The hero and the coward both feel the same thing, but the hero uses his fear, projects it onto his opponent, while the coward runs. It's the same thing, fear, but it's what you do with it that matters.*"

—Cus D'Amato, noted boxing trainer

CATHOLIC FAMILY RISK OWN LIVES TO HIDE JEWS FROM NAZIS

During World War II, Julian Bilecki and his cousin Roman, both Catholic teenagers, lived with their families in Zawalow, Poland (now Ukraine). In June 1943, several Jews had escaped from the Nazis and sought help from the Bileckis. Risking death for aiding Jews, the boys and their fathers, Genko and Lewko, built a bunker in the woods and for almost a year provided the Jews with food. During the winter, Roman and Julian brought food to the Jews by jumping from tree to tree so they wouldn't leave telltale footprints. In the spring of 1944, the area was liberated by the Russian Army. The courage and commitment of the Bileckis saved the lives of twenty-three Jewish men, women, and children. Julian, now in his eighties, lives in Ukraine while Roman, also in his eighties, lives in Rochester, New York.

For more information:
www.shoah.dk/Courage/Bilecki.htm

RETIREE SAVES PILOT
WHO CRASHED IN LAKE

Larry Hicks watched in horror as a single-engine plane crashed into a lake near his home in Troy, Alabama, in 2002. After calling 911, he hopped in his boat to the crash site and dived three times into the murky ten-foot-deep water until he found the unconscious pilot, Jack Roush, and brought him to the surface. Hicks gripped a wing with one arm and kept Roush's head above water with the other while spilled aviation fuel began smoking. Recalled Hicks, a retired Marine, "I thought it was going to blow up. I turned around and yelled to my wife [on shore], 'No matter what happens, Donna, I love you.'" Then he propped Roush on a wing and performed CPR until the pilot began coughing up water and blood. Hicks fought cramps in both arms until help came fifteen minutes later. Despite a severe head injury and multiple broken bones, Roush recovered. A deeply religious man, Hicks corrects those who say he acted alone. "No, *we* did a great job," he said. "Without the good Lord, Jack wouldn't be here."

SCHOOLBOY GETS PAL OUT OF ICY WATER

Richard Watt, eighteen, a physics student at St. Andrews University, thought it was a dumb idea for his pal Will Drury, also eighteen, to go for a midnight swim in the icy sea near Dundee, Scotland, in the winter of 2004. It was more than dumb. It was incredibly dangerous. Seeing his buddy begin to flounder in the freezing waters, Watt called emergency services on a cell phone, and then plunged into the sea to save his friend. Watt spent fifteen minutes holding Drury's head above water before getting him to shore, where they were met by emergency personnel. "Will had passed out and I was struggling to stay conscious," Watt recalled. "I thought we were both going to die. Then I saw flashing lights and that led me back to shore."

DISABLED DOCTOR OPERATES ON THE POOR FOR FREE

Despite health problems that left him seriously disabled, plastic surgeon Sharadkumar Dicksheet, of Brooklyn, New York, refused to give up. He continued to travel to his native India for six months each year to perform corrective surgery on those who couldn't afford it. He began his volunteer work in 1968 and continued even after he was partially paralyzed in a car accident in 1978. Since then he survived two severe heart attacks that left him unable to practice medicine in the U.S., but he continued operating on victims of deformities in India until 1998. "I see this as an entirely personal mission," he said before finally retiring. "I am pushing my luck. But that is exactly why I am here. To push my luck and the frontiers of endurance and do what I see as my duty, my job."

STUDENT PULLS INJURED DRIVER FROM BURNING CAR

Flames and a looming explosion didn't stop Ashley Roque from saving a life. In 2004, near St. Augustine, Florida, the Jacksonville University student saw a car lose control, crash into a tree, and burst into flames. Roque called 911 on his cell phone and then raced to the burning vehicle. The driver, Laura Beth Thompson, twenty-five, was covered in blood and cried, "I can't get out!" Both car doors were smashed in by the accident so Roque, twenty-one, reached through the broken side window. Although he feared she might have back or neck injuries, he couldn't wait. He put his arms under her armpits and dragged her out. He carried her on his shoulders and didn't put her down until they were across the road. Just then the car exploded. Thompson was taken to the hospital and treated for broken bones and a collapsed lung. Said Roque, "I did what I thought was right. I don't want to be praised."

"A hero is no braver than an ordinary man, but he is brave five minutes longer."

—Ralph Waldo Emerson, American poet

MAMA GORILLA DEFENDS FALLEN BOY

The crowd at the Brookfield Zoo in Illinois watched in horror as an unattended three-year-old boy climbed over a railing and fell twenty feet into the gorilla exhibit in the summer of 1996. They screamed for help as eight-year-old western lowland gorilla Binti Jua, carrying her baby Koola on her back, reached the unconscious boy. Gasps from the crowd turned to hushed amazement when the big ape gently picked up the toddler. She cradled him in her arms, shielding him from the other gorillas, and walked to the door where she knew the zookeepers would soon enter. Zookeepers, who took the child to safety, said her remarkable act was the result of her training in preparation for the birth of her baby. Binti Jua, whose name is Swahili for "daughter of sunshine," became an international celebrity for her heroic rescue of the boy, who recovered fully.

STUDENT CORNERS
BERSERK MURDERER

On his way to a softball game in Central Park in 2004, college student Anthony Jimenez carried his baseball bat into a Manhattan subway station. Moments later he used it to thwart a berserk murderer. According to police, earlier in the day Akeem Capers killed his grandmother in Brooklyn, then raped a neighbor before fleeing to the subway. Capers had just pushed another man onto the tracks when Jimenez encountered him. Capers tried to yank the bat out of Jimenez's hands, but the muscular twenty-year-old student, who worked in a health club, wouldn't let go. "I took one or two steps back and I got a grip on him and pushed him back," Jimenez recalled. "There was a short tussle. I went real low and I threw him up against a wall." Jimenez held Capers until police arrived moments later and took the assailant to a psychiatric ward. The man Capers pushed onto the tracks escaped without injury.

HERO FROM HISTORY
Susan B. Anthony

In 1872, a fifty-two-year-old spinster stepped into a voting booth in Rochester, New York, and changed history. As a crusader for women's suffrage, Susan B. Anthony, who was born on February 15, 1820, was convinced the U.S. Constitution granted women the right to vote. To test her theory, she voted in the presidential election and was promptly arrested, tried, and convicted of voting law violations. Anthony never paid the fine. For the rest of her life, she worked at grinding down laws and mores that treated women as second-class citizens. She never got to see the fruits of her lifelong work. The 19th Amendment to the Constitution, granting women the right to vote, passed in 1920, fourteen years after the death of this women's suffrage pioneer.

For more information: www.susanbanthonyhouse.org

YOUNG GIRL SAVES BOY IN POOL

At first, eleven-year-old Beth Dapper thought the small boy curled up at the bottom of the pool in Algonkian Regional Park in Sterling, Virginia, in 2004 was playing some kind of prank. Then she swam closer. "His eyes were rolled back, and it didn't seem normal," she recalled. "It freaked me out." But she put her fears aside and dove, grabbed his arm, and pulled the limp form to the surface. "It was scary, because I thought I was holding someone who was dead," said Beth. Once she got him to the surface, she draped his body over her shoulders and swam to the side, where a lifeguard performed CPR and got him breathing again. He was whisked off to a hospital where he recovered by the next day.

PET BIRD DIES
TRYING TO SAVE OWNER
FROM KILLERS

Apet cockatoo lost his life trying to protect his owner from a murderer, but he still helped convict the killer. In 2001, Daniel Torres attacked former boss Kevin Butler, owner of a pool company, in Butler's Houston home. After tying up the victim, Torres began stabbing and beating him, but then Butler's big white cockatoo, named Bird, flew onto the assailant and began pecking away. Torres killed Bird and then Butler, but police picked up samples of blood with Torres's DNA from Bird's beak. When he was arrested, Torres admitted that he stabbed Bird after he pecked him "all over my head." During Torres's trial, Prosecutor George West recounted Bird's heroism: "We know that this bird will attack anybody who is attacking his owner. And who did he attack? Daniel Torres." The jury convicted Torres of murder.

"Valor is a gift. Those having it never know for sure whether they have it until the test comes."

—Carl Sandburg, American poet

MOTORCYCLE COP
LEAPS ONTO RUNAWAY
LOCOMOTIVE

When he learned that a runaway locomotive was rolling through rural neighborhoods near Boise one day in 2003, Corporal Duane Prescott of the Idaho State Police hopped on his motorcycle and chased the engine. While officers raced from railroad crossing to railroad crossing to block traffic, Prescott leapt aboard the four-hundred-thousand-pound Union Pacific locomotive, then pushed and pulled every control he could find until it came to a stop. Police said Prescott halted the unmanned locomotive—which, at times, had been rolling downhill at about forty miles per hour—and prevented it from crashing into another engine sitting on the tracks farther ahead. "I was just the one who was lucky enough to be in the position to do it," said Prescott modestly.

PASSERBY SAVES WOMAN FROM BEING SWEPT OVER FALLS

In 2001, Andrey Sazonov and his wife, Galina, of Welland, Ontario, were walking along the Niagara River about five hundred yards from Horseshoe Falls when they saw a car veer off the road and plunge into the swift, frigid river. While Galina called 911, Andrey raced down to the river where the driver, a woman who later admitted she was trying to commit suicide, had managed to get out of her sinking car. But she was in shock and unable to swim well. Knowing that she would soon be swept over the falls, Andrey jumped into the river and, risking his life, brought her safely to shore. "I'm just glad I happened to be there," Andrey said.

TEEN SAVES
ELECTROCUTED WORKER

Scott Baer, sixteen, of Rock Island, Illinois, never thought that his summer job would make him a hero. In 1977, he was working with Bernard Rossi, sixty-two, who was steadying a cast-iron pipe suspended from a crane on a truck that was moving slowly down a dirt lane in a forest preserve. Unexpectedly, the truck's boom touched an overhead power line, causing Rossi to suffer an electrical shock so strong that he was frozen to the charged metal in a standing position. The crane was still in contact with the line because the truck had stopped. Thinking quickly, Scott ran up behind Rossi and very carefully extended his arms around Rossi without touching him. Then in one swift movement, Scott clasped his hands together and jerked Rossi free of the charged metal. Scott was knocked over by an electric shock from touching Rossi. Scott, who wasn't injured, said he was happy that he had saved a life. Rossi was hospitalized for electrical burns.

For more information: www.carnegiehero.org

WOMAN
DASHES THROUGH FIRE
FOR HORSES

When fire broke out in a Washington, D.C., stable one winter's night in 1896, there seemed to be no hope for the horses inside, until Mrs. B. F. Cranshaw sprang to the rescue. "Turn in the alarm quick and then come help me save those poor horses," she told her husband before grabbing a heavy overcoat and rushing out. Smoke and flames darted out of the windows and a crowd had gathered outside. No one offered to help as she struggled to pull the heavy doors open. Alone, Mrs. Cranshaw dashed into the stable, wrapped an overcoat around the first horse's head, walked him out, and handed the halter to her husband, who brought the animal into the alley. Then she grabbed her coat and stormed back into the blaze. Although the second horse put up a struggle, Mrs. Cranshaw led it to safety as well. As she exited the burning stable, the idle crowd burst into applause. Mrs. Cranshaw emerged from the fire without a scratch but her overcoat was singed beyond repair.

SHOT FIVE TIMES, PUPPY CHASES GUNMAN FROM HOME

Brandy may look like a Springer spaniel, but when her owner, Kendall Plank, looks at the dog, she sees something quite different—a guardian angel. In 1996, Plank was sleeping alone in her home in Tucson, Arizona, when the sound of footsteps woke her. She called 911, but just as she put down the phone, the intruder opened fire with a machine gun. That's when Brandy, then a nine-month-old pup, took charge. She grabbed the gunman's arm and wouldn't let go even as he pumped five bullets into her. Then the brave puppy chased him from the house. Incredibly, Brandy survived. Her heroics turned her into a celebrity, feted and honored with awards from the local sheriff to a huge dog-food manufacturer. But, most importantly, she earned the eternal gratitude of her mistress. "If it hadn't been for her, I wouldn't be here today," Plank said.

"When the first Superman movie came out, I was frequently asked, 'What is a hero?' My answer was that a hero is someone who commits a courageous action without considering the consequences...Now my definition is completely different. I think a hero is an ordinary individual who finds strength to persevere and endure in spite of overwhelming obstacles."

—Christopher Reeve, actor, spinal cord–injury victim, and activist

ANGLER MAKES LIFESAVING CATCH

While Anthony Joshua was fishing on the banks of the River Wye in Hertfordshire, England, in 2001, he was startled when he spotted a drowning man floating by. "Suddenly these arms rose out of the water," Joshua recalled. "I couldn't believe it when I realized it was a man. I knew I had to get him out. He was blue and shaking violently. I didn't think he had long to live." It took three casts, but Joshua finally hooked the man and reeled him in. His catch was a sixty-year-old man who had slipped and fallen into the frigid water while walking along the riverbank. He was close to death when Joshua snagged him and brought him to shore where the angler revived him and then summoned help. Paramedics said that another minute in the water would have proved fatal. "I'm just glad I was in the right place at the right time," Joshua told reporters. "The bloke is alive and I'm delighted I could help."

SEVEN-YEAR-OLD GRABS WHEEL, SAVES DAD

Latia Robinson, seven, knew exactly what to do when her father passed out behind the wheel in 1998 in rush-hour traffic in Washington, D.C. Latia looked over at her father, who was unconscious from a medical problem. So the second-grader pushed her dad into the passenger seat and got behind the wheel. At four-foot-four, she had to strain to reach the pedals as she carefully maneuvered the car to Howard University Hospital. She knew the way because her father had once driven her there. At the emergency room, she put the car in park, jumped out, and started banging on the ambulance entrance door. Doctors called Latia's actions "astonishing" and were certain her quick thinking saved her father. Latia was given awards and was praised by celebrities, including President Clinton.

MAN SAVES MOTORISTS FROM FALLING TELEPHONE POLE

At great cost to his own safety, Charles Gedney Jr. saved an untold number of persons from a falling telephone pole in Seattle in 1985. Gedney, forty-seven, a manufacturer's sales agent, was in the doorway of an office when he saw a wooden telephone pole that had been fractured in an earlier accident begin to sway. Believing the pole might fall onto the adjacent busy street, Gedney ran into the road, waving his arms to warn oncoming motorists. Several approaching vehicles screeched to a halt to avoid being crushed as the pole fell across the road. Unfortunately, Gedney was so busy warning others that he failed to get out of the way in time and was struck by the pole. Gedney was hospitalized for extensive injuries, including a fractured skull and broken vertebrae, but he said he was grateful no one else was hurt.

For more information: www.carnegiehero.org

CLEANING LADY BECOMES "DICTIONARY LADY"

In 1992, Annie Plummer, a fifty-five-year-old cleaning lady from Savannah, Georgia, was trying to start a campaign to get a traffic light and crossing guard at a dangerous intersection when she noticed something even more upsetting. "I saw all the children with no books," she said. With fifty dollars of her own money, she bought thirty pocket dictionaries and started passing them out. After a television news program ran a feature on her, Georgia opened its wallets. Plummer, who dropped out of school in ninth grade and never owned a dictionary as a child, became the "Dictionary Lady" and a shrewd fundraiser with T-shirts, walkathons, and thousands of young fans. By the time she died in 1999, more than thirty-two-thousand children had dictionaries thanks to Plummer. In each dictionary she handed out she wrote the motto of the United Negro College Fund: "A mind is a terrible thing to waste." Under that she added, "I challenge you not to waste yours."

For more information: www.dictionaryproject.org

CHEF JUMPS INTO FIRE
TO SAVE CRASHED PILOT

Nathan Michael Grube, a chef from Wind Gap, Pennsylvania, was driving near a local airport in 2002 when he spotted smoke and flames from a burning airplane that had missed the runway and crashed moments earlier. He ran to the burning wreckage where the pilot had escaped, but passenger William S. Smith Jr. was unconscious in the front left seat. Pulling his jacket over his head to protect himself from the fire in the cockpit, Grube reached in and pulled Smith to safety, seconds before the front half of the plane exploded.

TRAIN CONDUCTOR
GIVES LIFESAVING KICK

Conductor Bob Mohr saw something moving in the path of his 6,700-ton, 7,200-foot-long Norfolk Southern Railway train as it passed through Lafayette, Indiana, in 1998. "It's a baby!" he yelled to the engineer. Both knew it would be impossible to stop the train in time, so Mohr climbed down to the last rung of a ladder at the front of the engine. He leaned over, putting himself in position to snatch the girl as they passed. Hearing the noise, the child moved so she was just out of his reach, but still in danger. In the last terrifying moment, Mohr stretched out his right leg and aimed a good hard kick at the toddler. As the train moved on, Mohr leapt off, ran back, and heard a wonderful sound. "Mama, mama," the child was crying. Blood was streaming from a big gash on her forehead, but otherwise she was fine. Exhausted, Mohr gathered the child, nineteen-month-old Emily Marshall, in his arms and gave her to her relieved mother, who had been searching for the girl.

WWII GUNNER BEGS TO SACRIFICE LIFE FOR PLANE

As the crippled Flying Fortress lost altitude over the English Channel in 1944, twenty-one-year-old Tech Sergeant Forrest L. Vosler pleaded with the captain, "Throw me out…I'm hit badly and no use to you now…It'll save you one hundred seventy-five pounds and maybe get you back to England." Earlier during an air battle over Germany, a shell had shredded Vosler's eyes, chest, face, and legs. Nevertheless, working just by touch, he rigged an emergency radio set and tapped out "S-O-S," never stopping despite searing pain. As the crew jettisoned every excess pound to make it back to base, Vosler volunteered to sacrifice his life to lighten the load. But his comrades refused. When the plane ditched, Vosler, blind and bleeding, managed to rescue an injured tail gunner by pulling him out of the water and holding him onto the wing until both could climb into a dinghy. Six months later, with the best medical care, Sergeant Vosler's vision was partially restored and he was able to see President Roosevelt pin the Congressional Medal of Honor on his chest.

For more information on Medals of Honor:
www.cmohs.org

FARMER OPENS HEART TO RWANDA'S ORPHANS

Rosamond Halsey Carr, a former New York fashion illustrator, moved to Rwanda where she operated a flower plantation. She stayed even as conflicts between rival tribes the Tutsis and the Hutus drove every other white farmer from the region. In 1994, the hostilities flared into a bloody genocide that left one million dead. But Carr, at eighty-two, still refused to turn her back on her adopted country. She converted a building on her land into an orphanage for children whose parents perished in the fighting and named it Imbabazi, which means "a place where you will get a mother's love." More than one hundred twenty orphans were soon under her wing. Most were sick, traumatized, or mutilated, like the boy whose hands had been whacked off with a machete. In 2004, Carr celebrated her ninety-first birthday surrounded by the orphans of Imbabazi.

You can read more about Rosamond Carr in her autobiography, *Land of a Thousand Hills: My Life in Rwanda* (Plume).

STRAY MUTTS WARM LOST BOY THROUGH FRIGID NIGHT

Josh Coffey, ten, who has Down syndrome, was in his backyard in Cassville, Missouri, playing with two stray mutts on a cold March day in 1996 when he disappeared. More than seven hundred people searched for the boy, but everyone feared the worst after the wind chill plunged to 34 degrees below zero. Three days after Josh disappeared, one of the searchers spotted a mutt barking in the woods about a mile from the Coffey home. He followed the dog and found Josh lying face down with his coat over his head. Miraculously, the boy had survived, thanks to the two dogs, a blue heeler mutt and a dachshund-beagle mix. They saved his life by curling up beside him and keeping him warm. Josh recovered from his ordeal and the pups—named Baby and Angel—were adopted by his grateful family.

SKYDIVER SACRIFICES OWN LIFE TO SAVE STUDENT

What started as a routine skydive in 2002 ended with a fatal fall for Robert J. Bonadies, forty-seven, of Vernon, Connecticut, who gave his own life to save his student, Cynthia M. Hyland, forty-two. Bonadies, Hyland, and another instructor jumped out at twelve thousand feet, but as they passed the point where they were supposed to open their parachutes, they started tumbling rapidly toward the ground because of malfunctions. At two thousand feet, the other instructor broke away and opened his chute, but Bonadies stayed with Hyland as they plummeted to earth. With just eight hundred feet to go, Bonadies managed to open Hyland's parachute, saving her life. But he did not have time to open his own and died when he slammed into the ground.

For more information: www.carnegiehero.org

"Conscience is the root of all true courage; if a man would be brave let him obey his conscience."

—James Freeman Clarke,
nineteenth-century theologian

RETIRED NURSE BRAVES BULLETS TO SAVE TENANT

When seventy-four-year-old Marguerite Zachary heard gunfire, she didn't run for cover. Instead she rushed straight into the line of fire to save another. In 2002, Zachary was sitting in her apartment in the complex she managed in Dallas, Oregon, when shots rang out. Another resident, Charlotte J. Woods, fifty-nine, was on the ground, bleeding in the courtyard about sixty feet away. Zachary, a retired practical nurse, ran to Woods even though the gunman was still shooting from the balcony on the second floor. She knelt to tend to Woods and comforted the wounded woman until police arrived. After a five-hour standoff, police captured and arrested the assailant.

HERO FROM HISTORY
Harriet Tubman

Born a slave, Harriet Tubman threw off her shackles in 1849 and fled to freedom. Then in an act of remarkable courage, she began helping other slaves escape. Over the following decade, Tubman returned to the South again and again, leading hundreds of slaves—including her parents—on the Underground Railroad, a network of safe houses along the route to northern free states and Canada. At one time the "Moses of her people" had a bounty on her head of forty thousand dollars, but it didn't stop her. Throughout the Civil War, Tubman worked tirelessly to end slavery, aiding abolitionists and spying for the Union. When the South fell, Tubman was hailed as a hero.

For more information:
www.nyhistory.com/harriettubman/life.htm

DOG WARNS DEAF OWNER OF FIRE

Taj Brumleve was in a deep slumber when fire broke out in her Redmond, Washington, apartment one night in 1996. Ivan, a fifteen-month-old Labrador retriever–Siberian husky mix, knew just how to rouse his owner, even though Brumleve is deaf. Instead of barking, Ivan sounded the alarm by leaping on Brumleve and jumping up and down on her chest. Once Ivan was satisfied she was awake and on the move, the dog darted to the room where Brumleve's three-year-old daughter was sleeping and woke up the child, and led them both out the front door and to safety.

RETIREE PLUNGES INTO POND TO HELP FRIEND

Carolyn Kelly, a retired medical technologist from Shreveport, Louisiana, thought nothing of stripping off her clothes and leaping into a pond to rescue her friend, eighty-three-year-old Nina Hutchinson, in 2002. It didn't matter to Kelly that, at eighty-one, she herself was no spring chicken. Hutchinson was in a car that somehow rolled into the pond and started to sink. She freed herself, but was thrashing about in the water when Kelly arrived, having heard the crash from her home nearby. In a flash she ripped off her outer garments and dove in. When she got to Hutchinson, she moved her to the car and propped her against its side until firefighters brought them to shore one by one. Sadly, Hutchinson did not survive, dying at the hospital a day after Kelly's heroic water rescue.

GRANDFATHER
COLLARS GUNMAN

The sight of an armed thug threatening a bank guard was the last straw for a seventy-year-old grandfather in East Belfast, Ireland, in 2003. "I just couldn't stand by and watch this guy pointing a gun at another man," recalled the brave pensioner, who requested anonymity. A former cop and athlete, the man grabbed the robber from behind and after a fierce struggle, managed to get the crook in a headlock. The robber, Richard David McCarten, was later convicted and sentenced to eleven years in jail. "I had to take action," the hero told reporters. "This sort of thing is happening too frequently in this part of the world. I have seen elderly people being beaten and robbed, and I would never allow that to take place if I were in a position to stop it."

> *"Poets and heroes are of the same race; the latter do what the former conceive."*

—Alphonse de Lamartine, French poet, statesman, and historian

WIDOWER THWARTS JUMPER AT SITE OF WIFE'S DEATH LEAP

At six hundred thirty feet above sea level, Beachy Head is the highest chalk sea cliff in Britain and a prime tourist spot. But, as Keith Lane learned in 2004, it has a sinister side. Locals call the cliff Suicide Point because it's a favorite place for despondent jumpers. A week after Lane's wife, Maggie, leapt to her death, the grieving widower returned to Beachy Head, hoping the visit might help him cope with his tragedy. Instead he ended up preventing another one. On an early morning walk, he spotted a woman writing a note and asked what she was doing. She told him to beat it. "I can't do that," Lane said. At that moment she bolted. Lane ran after her. Just fifteen feet from the edge, Lane tackled the woman and held her down until police arrived. For saving the woman's life, Lane was honored with an award from Britain's Royal Humane Society. Determined to save even more lives, Lane set up the Maggie Lane Charity to fund round-the-clock patrols on Suicide Point.

ROTTWEILER
BARKS ALARM FOR
DANGLING WORKERS

Two Manhattan high-rise workers owe their lives to an alert nineteen-month-old Rottweiler named Boogey Baby. In 2004, the scaffolding holding two maintenance men five stories above the ground collapsed, leaving them dangling in their harnesses. No one heard their cries for help except Boogey Baby. The dog's owner, T. Jones, and his fiancée, Linda Bright, were watching television when the excited Rottweiler came charging into the room, barking loudly. "I knew there was something wrong when she dropped her bone," said Jones. He ran to the window and saw the two men yelling for help. Jones rushed downstairs and summoned rescuers who pulled the men to safety with a rope. "She is a heroine," said Bright, a dog trainer. "I love that dog even more now."

AIRMAN MAKES VALIANT EFFORT TO SAVE BUDDY

On a bombing raid near Nagasaki in 1944, the Superfortress *Heavenly Body* was riddled with enemy bullets. Flight engineer Harry Miller was wounded in the head while the pilot, Capt. Jack Ledford, was hit in the side, shattering his hipbone and exposing his spine. Ledford stayed at the controls, refusing morphine because he wanted to keep his head clear while he tried to guide the plane to friendly territory in China. When the *Heavenly Body* started going down, the pilot ordered everyone to bail. Miller was unconscious, so Ledford rigged a makeshift static line on Miller's parachute and tossed him out of the plane. Moments later, the chute opened and Ledford followed close behind, plunging nearly a mile in a freefall before pulling his ripcord in an attempt to hit the ground before Miller so he could catch him. His plan was foiled when wind separated them. Miller was still alive when Chinese soldiers found him, but he died later in a hospital. Ledford received the Medal of Honor for his daring plunge.

For more information on Medals of Honor:
www.cmohs.org

GARDEN ACTIVIST REVIVES SLUM

The abandoned lot in one of the worst areas of southcentral Los Angeles was an eyesore in 2000. Filled with rusting cars and rotting trash, the lot seemed only useful to the neighborhood's many drug dealers and prostitutes. But Maurice Jones saw something else—a perfect spot for a garden that would revitalize his crime-blighted neighborhood. He thought that if this forty-five-foot by one-hundred-nineteen-foot lot could be taken back and beautified, it would help change people's views about their community. Maurice and his wife, Diane, went to work writing grants, raising funds, and recruiting volunteers to till the soil and plant seeds. It was dangerous—lowlifes were not happy to see their stomping ground invaded by a bunch of do-gooders with rakes and shovels. But local cops started patrolling more often, forcing the criminals to find another playground. The once trash-strewn lot was replaced with vegetable patches where volunteers grow food for the poor. Best of all, in just one year, the crime rate dropped by more than 25 percent.

LIVE WIRE RESCUE

Retired Buffalo police detective Harold Ferguson suffered a heart attack while he was driving in 1998. His van careened into a utility pole, which fell across the front of the vehicle. Practical nurse Alexis McMahon, thirty-seven, was in her kitchen at the time. When the lights went out in her house, she looked outside. To her horror she saw the stricken driver with power lines draped across his wrecked van. Despite the danger of electrocution, McMahon and a neighbor, dentist Peter Purcell, pulled Ferguson from the van and stretched him out on the grass. McMahon couldn't find Ferguson's pulse, so she started CPR, working on him until firefighters arrived with a defibrillator. Doctors say that her actions saved Ferguson. "I got a new lease on life," he said later from his hospital bed.

> *"Cowards die many times before their deaths; the valiant never taste of death but once."*

—William Shakespeare, English playwright

HERO FROM HISTORY
Rosa Parks

By simply refusing to stand up on a bus, a forty-three-year-old African American seamstress from Montgomery, Alabama, lit the fuse in the long-simmering battle for equality and became known as the mother of the civil rights movement. But in 1955, she was just a tired woman heading home after a long day's work. All the seats in back, where blacks were forced to sit, were taken so she took a seat in the midsection. When the front seats, marked for whites only, were filled, the driver demanded that she give her seat to a white man. Parks continued to sit tight as the driver bellowed at her. When the bus driver called the police, she refused to budge, even as they arrested her for violating segregation laws. Her action led to a boycott of the Montgomery buses. It ended a year later when the Supreme Court declared segregation on public transportation unconstitutional—the ruling that would eventually give rise to the Civil Rights Act of 1964.

For more information:
www.achievement.org/autodoc/page/par0bio-1

Rosa Parks Library and Museum, Troy University
Montgomery: montgomery.troy.edu/museum

AIRMAN DANGLES FROM HELICOPTER IN ICE RESCUE

In 1979, a small plane crashed into Lake of the Woods in Ontario, leaving one of its occupants—Selma Irwin, forty-four—in the freezing water, clinging to a chunk of ice. A rescue helicopter rushed to the scene. With time running out before she died from hypothermia, airman Robert Grant, thirty-six, made the daring decision to pull her into the craft. The first try failed when Irwin, her hands too frozen to hold on, fell back into the water. Grant thought he lost her, but she bobbed up to the surface. To get a better grip on her, he needed both arms free, so he looped his legs around the skid and dangled upside down like a trapeze artist. Still holding onto Irwin's arms, he had the pilot fly to a thick sheet of ice where Grant released her and then jumped down on it. From there, he hoisted the woman into the helicopter. For their daring rescue, Grant and pilot Brian Clegg received commendations and Irwin's gratitude.

Suggested reading: *Rescue: Stories of Survival from Land and Sea* by Dorcas Miller (Adrenaline Books, 2000)

SHOW DOG'S VALOR
SAVES DROWNING BOY

Lucason of Ashtead O'Bellhaven, a collie with a long name and an even longer pedigree, was a champion in the show ring in 1935. But that same year, he proved he was more than just a pretty face. He was a hero. Anthony Salvatore, ten, was in a rowboat on New Jersey's North Shrewsbury River when it overturned. Anthony was floundering a hundred feet from shore, not far from the spot where the dog was being groomed for an upcoming show. Lucason leapt into the water and dog-paddled out to the drowning boy, grasped him gently by his clothes, and pulled him to shore. Anthony quickly recovered. The next day judges noted that the champion seemed a little worn by his ordeal, not quite on his winning form, but the beautiful dog still took home the blue ribbon.

PASSERBY SAVES WOMAN FROM SLASHER

In 2002, R. Johnson, a twenty-six-year-old apprentice electrician from Pittsburgh, was driving past the home of Wen Ting Huang, thirty, when he saw her being attacked by a man waving an eight-inch meat cleaver. Johnson bolted from his car and ran screaming at the man, who dropped his weapon and took off. After a short pursuit, Johnson grabbed him and pinned him against a wall until police arrived and arrested the assailant, who was charged with attempted murder. Recovered from several slash wounds, Huang said she was glad Johnson prevented her from becoming a murder victim.

MOUNTAINEER RESCUES INJURED CLIMBER ON EVEREST

David Swift, of Plymouth, England, was on an expedition tackling Mount Everest in 2004. At twenty-six-thousand feet, his group came upon two climbers in desperate trouble. One man had a broken leg. The other, Australian Peter Madew, was snow-blind, frostbitten, and dehydrated. While the rest of the group carried the man with the broken leg down on a stretcher, Swift volunteered to carry Madew, who could neither see nor use his hands down the treacherous slope. "I roped myself to him, and we set off down the mountain," Swift recalled. "Because of the wind, our fixed ropes had been blown away and at times there were two-thousand-meter drops on either side." It took seven harrowing hours, but Swift got Madew to Base Camp, where he was whisked to a Kathmandu hospital. The rescue meant Swift had to put off his lifelong dream of reaching the top of the world's tallest mountain (29,035 feet). "It was hard being so close to the summit and then having to turn back," Swift said. "But I did think if I was in the injured man's position, I would like someone to help me."

> *"Courage and perseverance have a magical talisman, before which difficulties disappear and obstacles vanish into air."*

—President John Quincy Adams

VACATIONING BRIT COPS COLLAR NEW YORK CROOK

It was a busman's holiday for a British couple—both police officers—when they snagged a violent criminal during the last day of their vacation in New York in 2004. Colin "Spike" Webber, thirty-seven, and his wife, Claire Webber, thirty-eight, were shopping for a necklace in the diamond district when they heard a commotion. According to police, street hustler Abraham Sariashvili had stabbed diamond dealer Arsen Arabayev, then took off. The sight of the man running and clutching a bloody knife sent Colin into action. He knocked Sariashvili to the sidewalk and held him down until local police arrived. Meanwhile Claire kept the crowd under control. The couple won a certificate of appreciation from the NYPD and a diamond pendant from a local newspaper, but the Webbers said they were "gob smacked" by all the attention. "You feel it's your duty, it's nothing out of the ordinary," said Claire. "Once you're a police officer, it's twenty-four seven."

MAN RESCUES DRIVER FROM SINKING TRUCK

While driving his pickup truck in 2002, Phillip H. Estes, sixty-eight, veered off the road and into the raging Yakima River near Richland, Washington. Unconscious behind the wheel, Estes was helpless as the current swept his pickup downstream. Seeing the drama unfold, David Brons, a thirty-one-year-old pipe fitter, jumped into the swift river and swam to the truck. He jumped onto the bed and tried futilely to smash the rear window of the cab. He called to bystanders on the bank who tossed him a rock, which he used to shatter the window. By now, the truck was sinking rapidly. Brons yelled to shore for a knife, which was tossed to him. He swam underwater and forced the driver's side door open. While standing on the running board to gain leverage, he cut the seat belt and hauled Estes from the truck to the surface. Estes spent two months in the hospital but eventually recovered from the ordeal.

PIG HELPS SAVE
INJURED OWNER

JoAnne Altsman was alone in her trailer on Presque Isle in Erie, Pennsylvania, in 1998 when she began to feel chest pains. "Somebody help me! Call an ambulance!" Altsman screamed. No one heard her. Her dog panicked, but thanks to an unlikely heroine—LuLu, her pet potbellied pig—Altsman, fifty-seven, survived. LuLu seemed to understand her owner's screams and dashed from the trailer, pushed open the gate, and rushed to the road. There she rolled over on her back and waved her hooves in the air until a driver stopped and followed her to the trailer where he summoned help. Altsman's doctors said that LuLu saved her life. Had help arrived fifteen minutes later, they said, Altsman would have died.

BANKER BATTLES GUNMAN TO SAVE COLLEAGUE

While Jerry Gibson was at his job at a bank in Harlan, Kentucky, in April 2002, he watched in shock as a gunman seized employee Jennifer Petrey, thirty-seven, and dragged her toward a utility room. Although unarmed, Gibson charged after the assailant and grabbed him, allowing Petrey to flee. The attacker then tried to shoot him. Gibson lunged for the gun and was locked in a life-and-death struggle for control of the weapon. It fired once, but no one was hit. Even though the assailant was biting Gibson's hands, Gibson wrenched the gun away and removed the bullets. He then lugged the man outside and turned him over to police before going to the hospital for treatment of multiple cuts and bites.

ANGLER KEEPS HIS COOL IN ICE RESCUE

Christopher Garon was enjoying a day of ice fishing on Lake St. Clair in Michigan in 2003 when he saw a fellow angler fall through the ice. A group of fishermen ran to help, but backed off when the ice started cracking beneath them. One would-be rescuer jumped into the water anyway and grabbed the drowning man but soon they both were overcome by hypothermia and unable to get out of the freezing water. Garon then dashed across the ice, tossed them a rope, and pulled with all his might. The ice began cracking at his feet, but Garon refused to let go and succeeded in pulling them out before the ice gave way.

LITTLE AUSSIE GIRL KEEPS DINGO FROM SNATCHING SISTER

"Dingo! Dingo!" screamed five-year-old Georgia Corke as a wild dog slipped through the patio doors and headed for the bed where her fourteen-week-old sister, Scarlette, was lying in a hotel room on Fraser Island, Australia, in 2004. Georgia placed herself between her sister and the dingo, moving back and forth to block its path every time it lunged for the infant. Hearing her screams, Georgia's parents rushed into the room and saw their daughter standing her ground in front of the snarling beast. "It was quite nasty. It stood its ground too," said Georgia's mother, Belinda. Her husband chased the dingo, which was probably attracted by the sweet smell of the baby's milk, out of the room. Dingos have been known to snatch and kill children. Three years earlier on the same island one of the wild dogs had mauled a nine-year-old boy to death.

GI'S SOLO ACT SAVES U.S. RIFLE PLATOONS

Corporal James Slaton, thirty-five, a former taxi driver from Gulfport, Mississippi, was the lead scout of an infantry unit sent to knock out Nazi snipers that had pinned two U.S. rifle platoons in a battlefield in Italy in 1943. Slaton ran ahead of his squad and jumped over a stone wall right into the first enemy machine gun nest. In a flash he whipped out his bayonet and killed one Nazi, then shot the other. With machine gun fire whizzing past him, Slaton dashed over open ground until he was close enough to toss a grenade into the second nest. Slaton moved on, wiping out the third nest with his rifle. "The whole action only took about an hour, but it seemed a lot longer to me," he later told the *New York Times*. His brave solo act, which saved the rifle platoons, earned him the Medal of Honor.

For more information on Medals of Honor:
www.cmohs.org

FOURTH GRADER TAKES DRIVER'S SEAT WHEN TEACHER FAINTS

Driving his students on a field trip in 2003, elementary school teacher Rodney Booth suddenly passed out from a medical condition as his car roared down a Denver highway at 70 mph. The car bounced off the guardrail twice and careened out of control. In the back seat, fourth-grader Sarah Harmon immediately jumped up front and grabbed the wheel. "Wake up, Mr. Booth!" the frantic girl shouted. Sarah managed to steer the car across two lanes of traffic and over a grassy patch before stopping on a dirt road. Then she found the teacher's cell phone and dialed 911. Meanwhile, the plucky girl kept the other frightened children calm until help arrived. Booth recovered, and gave Sarah an A for bravery.

NEIGHBOR DRAGS ELDERLY PAIR FROM HOME BLAST

In a flash, the building burst into flames after a gas leak sparked a major explosion at the Modesto, California, home of Katherine Maddox, eighty, and Wayne Maxwell, seventy-nine, in 2002. Maddox, seriously burned, was trying unsuccessfully to open the front door, when her neighbor, retired construction worker Steve G. Montelongo, sixty-two, kicked the door in and pushed her outside. Then he ran inside and found Maxwell in the kitchen. By that time, fire blocked the way to the front door and debris blocked the back door. Montelongo spotted another door and kicked that open, even though he was barefoot, having given his shoes to Maxwell. The house was destroyed, but thanks to their neighbor, Maddox and Maxwell survived.

PET DOG BECOMES HERO IN *TITANIC* TRAGEDY

A big black Newfoundland named Rigel, the pet of the first officer, was reportedly a hero on the ill-fated *Titanic*. After the ship hit an iceberg and sank on April 14, 1912, Rigel paddled around in the twenty-eight-degree water for three hours, looking for his master. According to newspaper accounts, the dog neared a lifeboat filled with freezing, exhausted survivors who were too weak to call out to the *Carpathia*, the ship that had sped to the scene. In the darkness the *Carpathia's* crew could not see the lifeboat floating directly in front of them. But then the crew heard a dog barking. It was Rigel, swimming in front of the lifeboat. Hearing the bark, the *Carpathia's* captain peered into the darkness and spotted the survivors. All were pulled to safety. If it had not been for the courageous dog, the *Carpathia* would probably have slammed into the boat. Sadly, although Rigel was also saved, he lost the one person who meant the most to him in the world. His master was never found.

> *"A hero is someone who has given his or her life to something bigger than oneself."*

—Joseph Campbell, scholar

TEN-YEAR-OLD HERO IN CANAL DRAMA

Only ten years old, Daniel Penden already knows what it's like to be a hero. While on an Easter trip to Edinburgh, Scotland, in April 2004, the Manchester, England, lad was feeding ducks along a canal when he heard screams and thrashing. Another boy—eight-year-old Ross Hunter—had tried to retrieve a toy he spotted in the water and had fallen in. When Daniel saw Ross "flapping around like he couldn't swim" and his head going under, Daniel knew he had to take action. "I ran to a little ledge and tried to grab him," Daniel recalled. "I got his arm and pulled him against the ledge and he pressed his feet against it and was able to get out." Daniel then escorted Ross to the boy's home where, the lifesaver recalled, "his mum thanked me very much."

HERO FROM HISTORY
Jim Lovell

Astronaut Jim Lovell was just a day away from realizing his dream of walking on the moon, but then disaster struck in April 1970. After a loud bang, his three-man spacecraft—Apollo 13—started rolling and spewing icy debris. "Houston, we have a problem," Lovell radioed NASA as systems on the ship went haywire. Lovell and crewmembers Fred Haise and Jack Swigert and the scientists on the ground at NASA started feverishly improvising, trying to figure out how to bring them home. It seemed hopeless. The astronauts endured freezing conditions, low oxygen, and sleep deprivation, but with near superhuman discipline, they made it back to Earth. Lovell said he never had time to be scared. "We just got really busy." And, while he has been lauded as a hero, he doesn't see his actions on Apollo 13 as anything extraordinary. "Look, the situation was forced on me, and I did my job," he told reporters.

Lovell wrote a book about the mission, *Apollo 13: Lost Moon*, which was later made into the hit film *Apollo 13* starring Tom Hanks.

HEROIC SLED DOG SERUM RUN PREVENTS EPIDEMIC

A diphtheria epidemic threatened the entire population of Nome, Alaska, in the winter of 1925. Dr. Curtis Welch knew that his patients—many of them children—would die without a shipment of fresh serum. But the port was icebound and the nearest railhead was almost seven hundred miles away. A blizzard was brewing, preventing bush planes from flying. Only sled dogs could do it. So mushers, many of them Native Alaskans, arranged a relay and set off into the night at temperatures of 60 degrees below zero across mountains, rivers, and the treacherous ice of Norton Sound. A brave dog named Togo led his team over three hundred fifty miles through storms, suffering terribly and with almost no rest. Especially heroic were renowned musher Leonhard Seppala and his lead dog, Balto, who undertook the treacherous and long final leg. Thanks to the heroic 674-mile serum run, the brave mushers and their dogs saved the town from a deadly epidemic.

FLIGHT ATTENDANT SAVES SURVIVORS OF PLANE CRASH

In April 1936, Nellie Granger, a flight attendant on a TWA airliner, became a hero after the plane she was on crashed into the side of a mountain near Uniontown, Pennsylvania. Eleven of the fourteen people on board, including the pilot and co-pilot and the mayor of Newark, New Jersey, were killed. Granger survived and was thrown 125 feet from the wreckage. Nearby were two passengers, alive and conscious but too badly hurt to move. Although seriously injured, the one-hundred-pound Granger dragged the survivors away from the burning wreckage. Then she went for help, groping through icy mist and bitter winds until she came to a country road. She staggered to the home of Mrs. Ray Addis and telephoned for help. "She had a great lump on her head and her legs were all cut and bruised and her clothes torn and burned," Addis recalled. "She said she had to get back to the wreck." Granger, a registered nurse, returned to the scene and tended to the injured passengers until ambulances arrived. Authorities said Granger's efforts saved the passengers' lives.

PLUCKY GRANNY
SNATCHES TOT
FROM DRAIN

New York hailed her as the Hero Gran after a gutsy seventy-year-old woman, just two weeks after heart surgery, leapt six feet down into an open storm drain to save her seventeen-month-old grandson in 2004. While little Dominick Chrostowski was playing in a Brooklyn park, he tumbled into a storm drain that was covered by a black plastic bag, and he sank in muck up to his nose. His grandmother Theresa first tried to get help from two men who were passing by, but they ignored her. So she jumped in herself, snatched the tot, and handed him up to a woman who came to help. Park department workers said vandals had apparently removed the drain cover. Theresa and little Dominick were taken to the hospital where checkups found they were none the worse for wear.

"To have no heroes is to have no aspiration, to live on the momentum of the past, to be thrown back upon routine, sensuality, and the narrow self."

—Charles Horton Cooley, sociologist

AFRICAN WOMAN WINS NOBEL FOR 30 MILLION TREES

Throughout Africa she is known simply as the Tree Woman. Kenya's Wangari Maathai started earning that sobriquet in 1977 when she planted seven trees on Earth Day. She began to wonder if planting trees could solve two of her country's biggest problems—impoverished women and ravaged forests. She soon launched a group called the Green Belt Movement, which is dedicated to teaching women how to plant trees. Over the years, Maathai was sneered at, even jailed and beaten for protesting her government's environmental policies. Her husband left her, but nothing stopped her. By 2004, when her efforts had resulted in the planting of 30 million trees as well as new measures to safeguard Africa's environment, Maathai finally won the recognition she deserved. The sixty-four-year-old environmental activist became the first African woman—and only the twelfth woman ever—to win the prestigious Nobel Peace Prize. When asked what's next for the Nobel laureate, Maathai said, "More trees. I will grow more trees."

For more information: www.greenbeltmovement.org

AUSSIE GIRL FREES HUNTER FROM CROC'S JAWS

In April 1982, a brave twelve-year-old Australian girl saved a big-game hunter from becoming a crocodile's dinner. Peta-Lynn Mann, five-foot-two and one hundred five pounds, had been boar hunting in the jungle with family friend Hilton Graham, twenty-five, when a twelve-foot-long reptile snapped its jaws shut on his left arm and dragged him into the water. Instead of running away, Peta-Lynn waded into the bloody water. "Hang on!" she yelled, as the crocodile started shaking Graham. She grabbed his right hand and pulled with all her might, as the croc dragged them both into deeper water. Suddenly, the crocodile loosened its grip. Peta-Lynn yanked her friend free from the jaws of death, pulled him to the bank, then drove him to a hospital. Peta-Lynn, who won an award for bravery, said that she felt very proud that she could help him, but, she pointed out, "It's nothing like the shame I'd have felt if I hadn't."

CAT ALERTS MOM WHEN BABY STOPS BREATHING

Bernita and Roy Rogers, of Fort Leavenworth, Kansas, desperately wanted children, but three of their babies had died at birth and they feared their dream might never come true. To the couple's joy, on the fourth try Bernita delivered a healthy baby girl, Stacey, in 1986. Six weeks later, Bernita put the baby into her crib for a nap and went into another room to relax. But her cat Midnight wouldn't give her a moment's peace. He kept jumping on her lap and scratching at her legs. Again and again, she shooed him away, but he kept coming back. Finally, he dashed into the nursery and started moaning. Alarmed, Bernita ran in to see what was bothering him. She gasped in horror when she saw Stacey, blue in the face, gasping for air. The little girl had gone into respiratory failure, the result of a viral infection. Because Midnight sounded the lifesaving alarm, Stacey was rushed to the hospital in time and made a full recovery.

BUS DRIVER FOILS
SUICIDE BOMBER

Tel Aviv bus driver Baruch Noyman saw a passenger fall and hit his head after trying to jump onto the rear door of the bus in 2002. Noyman stopped the bus and, along with a passenger who was a doctor, rushed to help the injured, bleeding man. While opening the man's shirt, Noyman noticed a wire and assumed that the man was wearing a pacemaker. But then he realized he was wrong. "He's a suicide bomber!" Noyman shouted to his passengers. "Run!" By now the injured terrorist was trying to break free but Noyman and the doctor pinned him down while everyone on the street scrambled for cover. When the street was empty, Noyman and the doctor ran for their lives. The terrorist bolted, and about forty yards from the bus, detonated the ten pounds of explosives that had been strapped to his body. One woman was killed in the blast, but Israeli police said the damage would have been "catastrophic" had it not been for the bravery of the bus driver and the doctor.

TRUCKER COMES TO
RESCUE OF COP
IN TROUBLE

In 1999, trucker David Zorn, forty-three, was driving along an interstate in Georgia when he spotted a police officer in trouble on the side of the road, struggling with a drunk who had him on the ground and was trying to grab his gun. Zorn pulled his 18-wheeler to the shoulder and, brandishing a flashlight, took off after the assailant. "Don't hurt me!" the drunk yelled when Zorn caught up with him and pinned him to the ground until the officer came with handcuffs. "I'm glad I could do my civic duty," Zorn told *U.S.News & World Report*, "and I would do it again."

"You gain strength, courage, and confidence by every experience in which you really stop to look fear in the face. You are able to say to yourself, 'I lived through this horror. I can take the next thing that comes along.' You must do the thing you think you cannot do."

—First Lady Eleanor Roosevelt

NEIGHBOR TACKLES
RAGING DOG, SAVES TWO

Retiree C. James Rospert, sixty-eight, rescued two young people from a crazed seventy-pound dog in Bellevue, Ohio, in May 2003. The dog had mauled a boy, then turned on its owner, Rachael Baughn, sixteen, biting her on the arms and legs. Hearing Rachael scream, neighbor Rospert put on a pair of thick leather gloves and ran to tackle the beast. The angry animal turned away from Rachael and attacked the trucker. Before police arrived, the savage dog gave Rospert three deep bites, which required surgery and left scars. But thanks to Rospert's brave actions, the boy and Rachael were spared further injury. The dog was put to sleep.

VICTIM TURNS INTO AVENGER

At five feet tall, Texan Frank Norfleet looked like a pint-sized *patsy to a* band of the country's most notorious con artists. But they learned too late that Norfleet was no pushover. The gang swindled the wealthy fifty-four-year-old rancher out of forty-five thousand dollars in 1919. So Norfleet grabbed his ten-gallon hat and six-shooter and told his wife, Mattie Eliza, he was off to hunt crooks. "Bring them in alive," she advised. "Any fool can kill a man." Norfleet got on the conmen's trail, which ended up being thirty thousand miles long. The manhunt took four years and cost seventy-five thousand dollars—about a quarter of a million dollars in today's money—but he tracked them down. Norfleet, who became known as the Little Tiger, received an honorary commission in the Texas Rangers. Over the next decade he bagged one hundred desperados until Mattie Eliza insisted he come home. He returned to his ranch and stayed there until his death in 1967 at the age of one hundred two.

TERRIER TESTIFIES
AGAINST CROOK
IN COURT

Rusty Bud was the canine pal of New York screen-writer Jack Barton Loeb. Late one night in 1937, Loeb heard the wire-haired terrier barking and found him chasing a burglar around the living room. The burglar dashed out of the apartment and scampered down the stairs and out the door—with Rusty Bud close on his heels. Loeb called police and then ran out in his pajamas to find his dog. Rusty Bud had cornered the burglar, Frank Lucca, in front of a nearby apartment building, snarling at the slightest move. "Call him off! Call him off!" the burglar pleaded. "He's been biting my ankles!" Only after police arrived did Loeb tell his valiant dog to relax. At Lucca's trial, Loeb brought Rusty Bud into court. The dog was placed on the prosecutor's table in front of the jury box and immediately started growling at Lucca, who decided to change his plea to guilty.

CYCLIST PREVENTS
RAPE IN PARK

Bridget Scarpinato was enjoying a bicycle ride in a Massapequa, Long Island, park in 1996 when she saw something odd. A man who had been riding a bike earlier was now on foot, running behind a nineteen-year-old female jogger. Scarpinato turned around and decided to follow the man from a safe distance. A few moments later, Scarpinato heard a scream. She pedaled to the sound of the voice and discovered that the man had dragged the girl into the bushes and was attacking her. "I went into a rage and just started screaming at him," the fifty-year-old cyclist told the *New York Times*. She scared off the would-be rapist, then quickly called the cops and gave a description that led to his capture. "I wasn't frightened," Scarpinato said. "Maybe I was stupid, but I would do it again."

PRIEST GIVES HOME, HOPE TO MEXICO'S URCHINS

In 1954, a street urchin was nabbed stealing coins from a church poor box in Cuernavaca, Mexico. Police were ready to haul the little thief off to jail when the priest, Father William Bryce Wasson, persuaded them to give him custody of the boy. A few days later, the police called again, asking him if he wanted to take another eight grubby young felons. Father Wasson said yes and at that moment decided that it was his calling to help the homeless Mexican children. He founded an orphanage—Nuestros Pequeños Hermanos (Our Little Brothers and Sisters)—that gave hope to thousands. By the year 2000, Father Wasson had set up NPH homes, schools, and medical clinics in Haiti, Mexico, Nicaragua, Guatemala, El Salvador, and Honduras, and had helped more than twenty-five thousand children. Many of these once hopeless youngsters became teachers themselves, carrying on the work started by Father Wasson. He has been honored with the Kellogg's Hannah Neil World of Children Award.

For more information: www.nph.org

BOY USES LIMB TO SAVE DROWNING PILOT

Eight-year-old Dustin Dishon, of Buford, North Dakota, spotted a small plane in trouble in 1997. Inside, bush pilot Dennis Safranek, forty-eight, was trying to land his Piper Super Cub seaplane in the Missouri River. Instead he crashed into a rock in the river. The plane tipped on its nose and sank, leaving Safranek struggling in the rushing river. Dustin saw the accident, grabbed a fallen tree limb, and started running along the bank after the struggling pilot. Finally, he managed to get close enough so that Safranek could grab hold of the branch. Dustin then hauled him to safety. "If it wasn't for him," Safranek said, "I wouldn't be alive."

TEACHER DISARMS
GUN-TOTING STUDENT

In 2000 in Berlin Center, Ohio, history teacher Linda Robb, fifty-one, heard a commotion in the adjoining classroom and went to investigate. She was shocked to find a disturbed twelve-year-old waving a loaded 9 mm semi-automatic pistol and demanding that the twenty sixth graders and their twenty-four-year-old teacher get down on the floor. Robb knew she had to think fast to prevent a massacre. She entered the classroom and told the boy, "I love you and I care about you." He walked to the doorway and Robb hugged him. "Give me the gun," she said. To her surprise, he did, ending a potential tragedy. "Those other kids were absolutely terrified," Robb later told *U.S. News & World Report.* "I was thinking he could kill me. But I had no Plan B, so it had to work." Since the incident, Robb has corresponded with the troubled youth, who now views her as a grandmother figure.

TEEN SPRINTS TO SAVE TODDLER FROM TRAIN

High school student Kassandra Jenne Guymon, seventeen, of Clifton, Utah, knew the small boy she spotted walking along a railroad track in 2002 didn't belong there. So she stopped at the nearest house, hoping to find out where he belonged. But before she could ask any questions, she heard the sounds of an approaching train. In a panic, Kassandra sprinted two hundred twenty-five feet to where the toddler was standing on the tracks—right in the path of an oncoming locomotive traveling at forty miles per hour. With the train about a hundred feet away, Kassandra leapt and grabbed the boy, pulling him off the tracks just seconds before the huge wheels rumbled by.

For more information: www.carnegiehero.org

AIRMAN HAS FLARE
FOR HEROISM

Airman First Class John Levitow, twenty-three, was on his one hundred eighty-first air combat mission as loadmaster for an attack cargo plane on a night mission near Saigon, Vietnam, in 1969. Levitow's job that night was preparing magnesium flares to be tossed out of the twin-engine AC-47 gunship, known as Spooky 71. Levitow had just handed a flare to the gunner, when a mortar shell rocked the plane. Shrapnel tore into the crew, and Spooky 71 went into a wild descent. While trying to pull a comrade from the open cargo door, Levitow, who was bleeding profusely from more than forty wounds, noticed a smoking flare that had been armed was rolling around the floor. A flare burned at 4,000 degrees and, if one ignited inside the plane, it could easily melt the walls of the fuselage. The plane was pitching and rolling while the pilot tried desperately to regain control. With just seconds before the flare ignited, Levitow crawled over to the device and flung it out the cargo door as the flare burst in a white-hot blaze. The plane made it safely back to base. Levitow, who flew twenty more missions, was awarded the Medal of Honor for saving Spooky 71.

For more information on Medals of Honor: www.cmohs.org

ONE-LEGGED MAN PULLS EIGHTY-YEAR-OLD FROM FIRE

Missing a leg did not stop a British man from helping a neighbor in trouble in 2003. When Philip Couch, thirty-four, of Devon, England, noticed that the house of his neighbor, Jessie Carter, eighty, was on fire, he hobbled over to the blaze, tossed down his crutches, and entered the burning home. He got down on his belly and crawled through thick, billowing smoke, which was only one foot above the floor. Even though his eyes were tearing so much he couldn't see, he managed to find the elderly woman. Then, following the voice of his wife who was outside, Couch pulled the elderly woman out of danger. Couch, who lost his leg to cancer at age twelve, said that he didn't consider himself a hero. "When I saw smoke, my brain just went into autopilot," he said.

"When the will defies fear, when duty throws the gauntlet down to fate, when honor scorns to compromise with death—that is heroism."

—Robert Green Ingersoll, nineteenth-century American statesman and orator

ADVENTURER SAVES COMRADE IN SOUTH POLE NIGHTMARE

Adventurers Colin Bodill, fifty-four, and Jennifer Murray, sixty-three, were attempting a round-the-world record in 2003 via the South and North Poles in a helicopter. But they flew into a horrible nightmare in Antarctica when the helicopter crashed in a blizzard. Despite a cracked spine and severe chest injuries, Bodill braved the fierce, freezing winds and pulled his unconscious copilot from the wreckage. He wrapped her in a sleeping bag and erected a tent to shield them both from the brutal weather—where temperatures had plunged to 50 degrees below zero—before collapsing from his injuries. They were rescued four hours later and flown to a hospital in Chile. Both recovered, and Bodill won an award from the Royal Humane Society for his lifesaving actions.

SPEED DEMON SAVES KIDS FROM RUNAWAY STEED

In 1907, a big bay horse hauling a heavy truckload of iron was spooked. It started galloping down a hill, right toward a group of school children who were crossing the street in New York City. Luckily, Patrolman Charles M. Murphy was on the beat. Years earlier he became world famous as "Mile a Minute" Murphy by bicycling behind a speeding locomotive at sixty miles per hour. Now, Murphy would demonstrate the same strength and iron will. He shooed the children away and placed himself in the path of the runaway, which had no bit or reins. As the steed galloped by him, Murphy took a flying leap, threw his arms around the animal's neck and held on. Murphy kept squeezing its neck, trying to cut off its air supply. Finally the horse weakened and came to a stop. Murphy then calmly led it back to its owner and, without a word, returned to his beat.

DOG TAKES BITE OUT OF ATTACKER

"I'm gonna cut you, I'm gonna kill you," the assailant snarled as he held a knife to the throat of twenty-five-year-old ex-model Carina Schlesinger. The Danish-born beauty had been walking her dog Cookie, a fifty-pound German shepherd mix, in Central Park in May 2004 when the creep grabbed her, pulled out a knife, and started punching and choking her. Schlesinger put up a fierce struggle, kicking her assailant so hard he went flying. Meanwhile, Cookie sprang into action. Teeth bared, he leapt on the attacker, giving him three hard bites before the man fled into the bushes. Cookie not only saved his mistress, but he helped catch the criminal because the assailant's blood on Cookie's fur provided important DNA evidence. Said Schlesinger, who adopted the dog from a New Jersey pound four years earlier, "Cookie is my hero." Several months later the dog was given an award for bravery by the North Shore Animal League America.

For more information: www.nsalamerica.org

WOMAN RESCUES BURIED QUAKE VICTIMS

While Ruth Millington, thirty-four, a lawyer from Sheffield, England, was on a vacation in Bam, Iran, in 2003, an earthquake measuring 6.3 on the Richter scale leveled her hotel and 80 percent of the town. Miraculously she was not hurt and managed to claw her way out from under the debris. When she heard screams, she started hunting for victims buried in the rubble. Periodically rocked by aftershocks, Millington continued digging with her bare hands. "There was no emotion in it," she recalled. "I just thought I've got to get these people out." It took five hours for her to free one man who had been trapped under a concrete slab. Her hands scratched and bleeding, Millington managed to free ten victims. Seven survived. Millington said the experience changed her life. Once home, she established the Action for Orphans charity to help the three thousand children who lost everything in the nightmare quake, which claimed more than twenty-six thousand lives.

For more information: www.actionfororphans.co.uk

DRIVER STOPS UNCONSCIOUS MOTORIST'S RUNAWAY CAR

While driving on Interstate 75 in Cincinnati in 1984, Arthur Naltner, a forty-two-year-old salesman, was startled to see a piece of metal fly off the back of a truck and crash through the windshield of the motorist in front of him. The driver, Charles Snowdy, twenty-five, was knocked unconscious by the impact. However, his car continued traveling but was now out of control at about forty-five miles per hour. The quick-thinking Naltner maneuvered his subcompact auto in front of Snowdy's full-sized car until the bumpers made contact and then by braking, he brought both cars to a stop. Snowdy recovered from his injuries.

For more information: www.carnegiehero.org

> *"Most of us have far more courage than we ever dreamed possible."*

—Dale Carnegie, motivational speaker

HERO FROM HISTORY
Bill Wilson

After seventeen years as a drunk, Bill Wilson had an epiphany that would change his life—he gave up drinking. But five sober months later, when a business deal fell through in Akron, Ohio, he wanted a drink. Wilson thought if he could help another alcoholic, perhaps he could save himself, so he called an alcoholic friend. They talked for hours, Bill stayed sober, and his friend soon quit booze. That day led to the founding of Alcoholics Anonymous and Wilson's revolutionary twelve-step program, which has become a successful remedy for millions of alcohol abusers.

For more information:
www.alcoholics-anonymous.org

PIT BULL PROVES NO MATCH FOR COURAGEOUS CAT

Sparky, a four-year-old calico cat, turned into a raging lioness and rescued a helpless poodle from a pit bull's deadly jaws in 1989 in Dora, Alabama. Sparky's owner, Teresa Harper, had just let her poodle, Lacy Jane, outdoors when she heard a roar and saw a savage pit bull mauling her pet. From a porch ten feet away, Sparky gave a hiss, then leapt, scratching and clawing, onto the attacker's head. Bucking like a bronco, the pit bull finally threw Sparky off and ran away. Lacy Jane suffered several deep bites but recovered and owed her life to the courageous kitty.

FIREFIGHTER'S ROPE TRICK SAVES STRANDED CRANEMAN

Atlanta construction worker Ivers Sims was trapped atop a crane two hundred fifty feet over a blazing building in 1999. There was no way for firefighters to reach him from the ground. Unless something was done quickly, he would burn to death or the crane would melt, causing him to plunge to his death. So in a daring maneuver, firefighter Matt Moseley, thirty, swooped down from the sky. Dangling eighty feet at the end of a rope from a helicopter, Moseley flew over the raging inferno, then dropped onto the crane, and crawled to Sims. "Hey, your boss sent me up to tell you that you can knock off early today," the firefighter quipped. Moseley quickly hooked his own harness to the frightened Sims and signaled for the helicopter to take off, and the two men were whisked to safety.

SHOT MARINE SAVES TRUCKER FROM GUNMAN

Tow truck driver Brian Naylor, twenty-three, spotted a man next to a dilapidated Cadillac stuck on the side of California's Interstate 5 in 2002 and stopped to ask if he needed assistance. Inexplicably, the motorist, Henry Ricardo Enciso, twenty-six, flew into a rage, whipped out a gun, and started firing. Hit six times, Naylor staggered toward the highway, waving wildly for help, but no one even slowed down. But Marine Lance Corporal Trevor Farley, who was attending a meeting in a nearby base chapel, heard the gunfire. Farley sprinted one hundred yards to the wounded man, even though Enciso kept firing. Farley was shot twice, but he still managed to carry Naylor to safety. Enciso refused to surrender when police arrived and was shot dead. Ironically, Farley was in the chapel that day for a discharge meeting because a bad knee had made him unfit for duty. "I just saw someone in need, so I reacted to the situation," the Marine said. "At the time I wasn't concerned about myself."

NONSWIMMER SAVES
SUBMERGED DRIVER

Poor swimming skills didn't stand in the way of a daring water rescue in May 2003 after Ann Adamski's car plunged into a canal in Port Richey, Florida. Tracy Olson, a forty-one-year-old laborer, witnessed the accident and called police before grabbing a hammer and rushing to the aid of the eighty-seven-year-old driver who was trapped in the sinking car. Olson couldn't swim very well, so he dog-paddled twenty feet out to the car, which was nose first in eight feet of water. With the hammer, he broke through the rear window on the driver's side and crawled in headfirst and released Adamski's seat belt. She crawled to the back seat, where Olson pulled her free of the sinking vehicle. Adamski was also a weak swimmer, but together they struggled to the bank of the canal.

ONE-MAN ARMY POUNDS NAZI GUNNERS

When heavy Nazi machine gun fire pinned down his platoon, scrappy Technical Sergeant Nicholas Oresko, twenty-eight, of Bayonne, New Jersey, took matters into his own hands on a German battlefield in 1945. Oresko, five-foot-four and one hundred fifty pounds of pure fight, dashed out alone and tossed a hand grenade in the enemy nest, then finished off the Nazis with his rifle. A bullet wounded him in the hip, but still he ran on, toward a second Nazi bunker, constantly firing his rifle until he got close enough to toss another grenade and wipe out the rest of the German gunners. Oresko was in the hospital when he learned, to his surprise, that his attack had earned him America's highest military award. "All hell breaks loose, you do something—by instinct, I guess—and the next thing that happens is you hear you've won the Congressional Medal of Honor," he told the *New York Times*.

For more information on Medals of Honor:
www.cmohs.org

THREE CLIMBERS RESCUED IN DENALI DRAMA

In late May 1999 in Alaska's most treacherous mountain range, three British climbers were clawing their way up the sheer West Rib of Denali, the highest mountain in North America. Suddenly, a fierce storm slammed into the mountain and trapped the climbers at nineteen thousand feet. In whiteout conditions, helpless and suffering from hypothermia and dehydration, the climbers thought they were doomed. That's when U.S. Air Force's 210th Pararescue Squadron sprang into action. These parajumpers, known as PJs, were part of a thirty-man elite mountain team trained to rescue civilians. Risking their lives, the PJs battled the deadly elements in the hellacious storm and finally reached the trapped climbers and brought them out alive.

You can read more about the rescue in *The Rescue Season: The Heroic Story of Parajumpers on the Edge of the World* by Bob Drury (Simon & Schuster; 2001).

MOTHER TURNS PERSONAL TRAGEDY INTO QUEST FOR CURE

In 1996, when Jordana Holovach's six-month-old son Jacob was diagnosed with a rare genetic brain disorder called Canavan disease, she cried. But Holovach, of Westchester, New York, decided to try to use her own heartache to help find a cure. She became an activist, establishing the foundation Jacob's Cure and personally raising more than a million dollars for research into the causes of the incurable disease. She has testified before Congress, and her tireless lobbying helped secure a $2.3 million research grant from the National Institutes of Health. Jacob can't walk, talk, or lift his head, but he has benefited from some of the fruits of the research his mother helped to fund. A gene therapy procedure has improved his quality of life. "I'll never lose hope because I believe we can find a cure for the disease," she said.

For more information: www.jacobscure.org

SUBWAY RIDER AIDS SHOOTING VICTIM

First there was the sound of gunshots, then a woman's voice. "My arm, my arm! Somebody help me!" screamed Monica Meadows, twenty-three, a stunning model who had been riding the subway in New York City on July 6, 2004. Most of her fellow passengers fled in terror when a scruffy blond man shot the willowy blue-eyed brunette as the train neared Times Square. But rider Ashley Ruprecht, twenty-four, rushed toward her, even though the attacker was still on the loose. "I was afraid the gunman would come back. I kept looking around," she told the *New York Post*. "But I didn't want this girl to bleed to death." Rupert wrapped a sweatshirt around the wound and pressed with all her might. "I was worried for myself," she said, "but I was thinking if this was me, I would really want someone to help me out." Although the attacker got away, Ashley was relieved to know that thanks to her lifesaving measures, Meadows recovered from her injuries.

LAPDOG HELPS RESCUE OWNER IN CAR WRECK

One rainy night in 1996, Dusty, a two-year-old Bichon Frise, was riding in a car driven by her owner Joel Ward of Ely, Minnesota, when the vehicle skidded off a slick highway and tumbled down an embankment into a forest. Ward was injured and stuck inside, but miraculously, Dusty, who had been thrown from the car, was not hurt. She knew that her master needed immediate help. So the fluffy little white dog ran through the woods to the highway. Remaining in the middle of the road, she bounced up and down until someone stopped. Then, making sure the people were following, she led them to Ward's wrecked car and refused to move from his side until rescuers came to take him to the hospital.

FLIGHT ATTENDANT QUASHES HIJACK PLAN

Qantas purser Greg Khan saw the passenger coming at him with a sharp wooden stake shortly after takeoff of Flight 1731 from Melbourne, Australia, in 2003. "You're not getting to the flight deck," Khan, thirty-eight, said. The would-be hijacker, forty-year-old David Mark Robinson, grabbed Khan and started stabbing the back of his head again and again. Khan was so determined to keep the man away from the cockpit that he didn't even realize he was bleeding profusely from four large gashes in his head. Khan wrestled Robinson to the floor. Along with several passengers and another flight attendant, Khan kept Robinson restrained until the pilots could make an emergency landing in Melbourne.

The brave purser made a quick recovery from his wounds and was grateful no one else got hurt.

JOGGER SPRINTS TO AID OF SEIZURE VICTIM

Rob Carney was about to take a jog around a golf course in Aspen, Colorado, in 2004 when a frantic woman ran up to him. "My boyfriend had a seizure and drove his car into the lake!" she screamed. After running to a pond where the car, with the man inside, was nearly submerged, Carney yelled at the driver to roll down the window, but he just stared ahead with glazed eyes. Carney grabbed a rock, charged into the water, and smashed the window. But the man was so disoriented he didn't realize Carney was trying to help. Finally Carney seized the man's collar and hauled him out, then swam to shore. Moments later the car sank completely. The driver, who had never suffered a seizure before, was treated and soon released from the hospital. "I had to do it, there was no question. The poor guy was helpless," Carney told the *Aspen Times*.

KITTEN BATTLES RATTLESNAKE

Without her glasses, Johanna Tanner of Lompoc, California, couldn't see well, so she moved in for a closer look when she heard a strange rattling sound in her family room. As she stepped forward, her cat Ito rammed into her ankles. Barefoot, Johanna continued forward until Ito blocked her path. By now Tanner saw that a rattlesnake had entered the house. The cat then attacked the snake, but the reptile struck back and bit the brave feline on the right front paw. Tanner scooped up Ito and yelled for her husband, Roger, who then killed the snake. The fearless feline eventually recovered from the bite. "I just can't help thinking what would have happened if Ito hadn't seen the snake," Tanner said of the 1994 incident.

You can read about more heroic cats in
Mews Items: Amazing but True Cat Tales
by Allan Zullo and Mara Bovsun
(Andrews McMeel, 2005).

PERFECT CAST CATCHES DROWNING CHILD

Armand Grenot was jolted by the screams of children one day in 1961 as he stood fishing from a bridge over the Cher River in Tours, France. He looked down on the riverbank to a horrifying sight—a toddler had fallen into the rushing water and was being swept downstream. No one could reach three-year-old Claude Latapy. Two men dived in but couldn't get near him in the swift current. In a flash, Grenot figured that little Claude had just one chance of survival. "I knew I had to fish him out," recalled the expert angler. With one perfect cast, Grenot managed to snag the boy's jacket. Carefully Grenot reeled him in, walking off the bridge to the riverbank where bystanders pulled the boy to safety. Claude was unconscious but was quickly revived. "I won't ever have a more important catch in my entire life," Grenot said.

DOCTOR SAVES COLLEAGUE FROM CRAZED PATIENT

In 1995, Dr. Anthony Inwald was called upon to perform a lifesaving feat that had nothing to do with medical science and everything to do with courage. While making his rounds at a London hospital, he heard a commotion in a room where another doctor had been examining a woman who had a history of mental illness. When she started acting erratically, the doctor activated the hospital's internal alarm. Inwald ran into the room to help his colleague, but then the woman, who was clenching a large carving knife, began flailing away at Dr. Inwald. He battled the deranged woman, who stabbed him several times in the back, before he finally disarmed her and held her for police. Dr. Inwald was seriously injured and needed two months before returning to his regular lifesaving duties at the hospital.

"*A hero is one who does what he can. The others don't.*"

—Romain Rolland, French author

CAMPER SAVES GIRL FROM FALLING TREE

A 1990 family camping trip for Claude Saunders Jr. turned into a bittersweet day—he suffered severe injuries while saving a life. Enjoying the great outdoors in a wooded campground near Sweet Home, Oregon, Saunders, twenty-six, noticed that a two-hundred-foot-tall fir tree began to fall toward a campsite where Majesta Tatum, four, was playing. He raced over to her and pushed her out of the way a split second before the tree crashed down on him. Saunders was knocked to the ground, his right leg severed below the knee. Struck by branches, Majesta required hospitalization for two broken legs and other injuries, but she was saved from death. Saunders was hospitalized a month for his injuries, which included fractures to his pelvis and both legs.

HOOPS STAR HERO TO
CAR CRASH DUO

University of Florida basketball star Jimmy Baxter proved he could be a hero on and off the court. One rainy night as Baxter was driving home along a road in St. Petersburg in 2002, he saw a car skid and flip over into a ditch. Trapped upside down in the smoking car were Narcia and Ernesto Pavlov, a father and son who had recently emigrated from Bosnia. Putting aside his fears of an explosion, Baxter pulled over and ran to the wreck. "Help, help us please!" screamed Ernesto, as he beat against the mud-streaked windows. The doors were jammed. Baxter tried to kick in the window, but it wouldn't break. Then he ran out into the road and waved down a motorist who had a crowbar in the trunk. "God made me understand what I had to do," Baxter said later. Swinging the crowbar like slugger Alex Rodriguez, Baxter shattered the window and pulled the Pavlovs to safety.

MILITARY HORSE
BECOMES WAR HERO

Staff Sergeant Reckless was a racehorse that became a hero during the Korean War. She joined the 2nd Battalion, 5th Regiment of the First Division of the Marines when an officer purchased the Korean track star from a stable boy who needed money to buy an artificial leg for his sister. The military trained her to carry ammunition, and—despite her habit of raiding the chow tent and a weakness for beer, cola, and poker chips—the four-legged Marine served with distinction as an important member of the gun crew. "Every yard she advanced was showered with explosives. Fifty-one times she marched through the fiery gantlet of the Red barrage—and she saved the day for the Leathernecks," wrote the battalion's commander, Lt. Col. Andrew Geer in a book on the heroic horse, *Reckless, Pride of the Marines*. Reckless stayed behind when the Marines returned home, but a series of articles Geer wrote in the *Saturday Evening Post* spurred a movement that brought her to the U.S. The decorated war hero spent the rest of her life as a mascot at the Marine Corps base in Pendleton, California.

NEIGHBOR SAVES WOMAN FROM BERSERK HUBBY

Graham Tate, forty, was at his home in Somerset, England, in 1998, when he heard his neighbor's children shrieking in terror. "Papa's going to kill Mother!" the panicked kids wailed. Tate bounded over to the house, peered in the kitchen window, and saw a horrible scene. Tate's neighbor was holding his wife around the neck and pouring a can of gasoline over them both. Tate rushed into the house and grappled with his neighbor, allowing the woman to break free. During the struggle, the neighbor tossed gasoline over Tate and, with a cigarette lighter, set them both ablaze. Tate and the attacker suffered serious burns before firefighters arrived to help.

SWIMMER SAVES
DROWNING TRIO

Kevin D. Scheirer, a twenty-year-old canoe service driver, was floating in the Delaware River, near Bushkill, Pennsylvania, in 2002 when he heard a commotion downstream. Swimming toward the noise, he spotted two men and a boy thrashing wildly in the deep water, about fifty feet from the riverbank. Moments earlier, the boy, Alex Porres, twelve, had waded into water over his head. His father, Giovanni, thirty-six, dove in to save him, even though he couldn't swim. Alex's uncle, Rodolfo Colon, twenty-seven, rushed in to rescue Giovanni, but started floundering himself. Scheirer reached Alex and pulled the gasping child to the arms of waiting family members on the bank, then rescued the boy's father Colon had slipped under the surface by the time Scheirer went back the third time, but that didn't stop him. He dove under the water and grabbed the drowning man and towed him to safety.

For more information: www.carnegiehero.org

"Nurture your minds with great thoughts. To believe in the heroic makes heroes."

—Benjamin Disraeli, British statesman, prime minister, and writer

CLERK COMES TO AID
OF COP

While Jeffrey Mumford, thirty-seven, was at his job as a shipping and receiving clerk in St. Louis in 2002, he heard screams. Outside on the street he saw police officer Agatha Santangelo, thirty-eight, locked in a desperate struggle. Moments earlier, the officer had taken a knife from a suspect and was questioning him when he punched her, knocked her to the ground, and tried to grab her gun. He had her pinned when Mumford bolted to the scene, leapt on the attacker, and pulled him off the injured cop. Then Mumford held the man down until Officer Santangelo cuffed him. The officer, who required hospitalization and physical therapy to recover from the vicious attack, said she was grateful that Mumford had come to her rescue.

NEIGHBOR PULLS FIVE-YEAR-OLD FROM BURNING HOUSE

From his police and fire scanner, auto mechanic Joseph Wayne Wallace, of Tallahassee, Alabama, learned that fire had broken out in a nearby home and that five-year-old David Lawrence was missing. Wallace rushed to the scene and dashed through the front door. "David! David!" he called out, unable to see through the dense smoke filling the room. When the boy answered, Wallace followed the frightened voice through a burning hallway to the bedroom where he had to knock down the door. Finding the cowering boy under the bed, Wallace grabbed the child. A piece of burning ceiling crashed down on them while Wallace crawled through the fire to the front of the house, but the pair made it to the street and safety in the 2002 drama.

PET DOG SNIFFS OUT OWNER'S FAILING HEART

Steven Boyle of Narragansett, Rhode Island, was feeling tired during a three-week period in 2003. But it was only after his dog Grommett started acting unusual—circling and leaning on him and refusing to leave his side—that Boyle decided to take action. "He made me so uncomfortable that I decided to go to the hospital, and I was diagnosed with congestive heart failure," Boyle told a *Narragansett Times* reporter. He had contracted a virus that had infected his heart muscle and made it swell to three times its normal size. Doctors caught the condition in time to save Boyle. Grommett, a golden retriever he had adopted from a shelter in 1998, had demonstrated his diagnostic skills once before. A few years earlier, he showed the same strange behavior of circling, this time around Boyle's college-age son Francis. When the young man went to the doctor, he was diagnosed with mononucleosis.

BUS DRIVER SAVES STUDENT ON LAST DAY OF SCHOOL

For thirteen-year-old Jessica Lesson of Mechanicville, New York, the last day of school in 2000 might have been her last day on earth without the quick actions of a bus driver. Jessica was sucking on a lollipop on the school bus when suddenly the candy broke off the stick and slid down her throat, choking her. Bus driver Maria Hopeck slammed on the brakes and rushed over to Jessica. The girl's eyes were rolling back into her head, Hopeck recalled, and she was shaking violently. The bus driver pulled Jessica off the bus and attempted the Heimlich maneuver, but it didn't work. She tried again, and still the lollipop wouldn't budge. Finally with a third, frantic effort Hopeck dislodged the candy. Jessica recovered fully from the ordeal. "I really appreciate how she saved my life," the girl said. "I don't know how to tell her thank you."

ECONOMIST DEVOTES LIFE TO POOR TOWN IN INDIA

For twenty years, D. D. Choudhary had known the good life in America, pursuing advanced degrees in petroleum engineering and economics. So friends thought he had gone insane when he decided to put his credentials to use, not to make a killing in business, but to better his tiny hometown of Pothia, a hamlet of twelve hundred people deep in rural India with no roads, schools, post office, banks, or hospitals. All that Pothia had in abundance was ignorance and grinding poverty. Choudhary built a tiny school for six pupils. Then he continued building other facilities. Thanks to his efforts, today there are two schools (one for boys and one for girls), a post office, a bank, and a hospital. Best of all, Choudhary has wiped out illiteracy in Pothia by requiring that each of his students teach two adults to read.

COWORKER OFFERS
GIFT OF LIFE TO
KIDNEY PATIENT

Cindy Warner, a business manager for Catholic Charities in New York, read an email in the summer of 2004 asking if any employee would donate a kidney to a dying coworker. Mary Jane DiPaolo had been suffering from a rare kidney disorder for years. Her only hope was a donated kidney, but the transplant waiting list was so long she had little chance of getting one in time to save her life. So Warner stepped forward, and when tests confirmed she'd make a good match, doctors performed the transplant operation, which turned out to be successful. "I have two [kidneys] and she needed one," Warner later told the *New York Post*. When DiPaolo's doctor called Warner's donation "a rare but beautiful act of kindness," DiPaolo said, "How do you thank somebody for a kidney? I've come to the conclusion that you really can't. Her reward will be in a far better place than here."

PASSERBY SAVES DROWNING BOY

Rob Sharrow was strolling in Belle Isle Park, Michigan, on Memorial Day 2002 when he saw a boy thrashing wildly in the river. The boy had fallen off a fishing pier, the boy's frantic father shouted, and neither he nor his son could swim. Wasting no time, Sharrow threw off his shoes and shirt, dove into the cold water, and snatched the boy. But then strong currents swept the pair down the river. As Sharrow floundered, rapidly getting weaker, he noticed a metal bar hanging from another pier. Clutching the boy with one arm, he reached up and grabbed the metal bar with the other and held tight until bystanders pulled both out of the water.

TERRIER DRAGS
PARALYZED PAL
FROM FLAMES

Paralyzed from the shoulders down, Keith Chandler of Churchfields, England, was trapped in his bedroom after fire broke out in the kitchen of his home and spread throughout the house in 2003. His four small children bolted to safety through the front door, leaving him alone—or so he thought. As the room filled with thick black smoke, Chandler, twenty-nine, shouted for help, then managed to roll off the bed and wriggle toward the door, but his progress was slow and the house was rapidly turning into an inferno. Just then he felt himself being tugged by Sandy, his three-year-old Staffordshire terrier. The dog had been safe outside, but ran into the blaze when he heard Chandler's desperate cries for help. The dog pulled the paralyzed man through the patio doors and into the garden. "Another minute and I would have been a goner," a grateful Chandler later told the BBC.

HERO FROM HISTORY
Lech Walesa

An electrician from a Polish shipyard played a major role in short-circuiting communist rule in Europe. Lech Walesa was just one of many discontented workers at a shipyard in Gdansk, Poland, in the 1970s. In 1980, he led a strike that gave birth to Solidarity, the first independent trade union in the Soviet bloc, with Walesa as its head. Soon Solidarity had the support of 10 million people, representing most of the workforce of Poland. The government clamped down, declared Solidarity illegal, and arrested Walesa. Solidarity went underground and refused to die. After widespread strikes in 1989 forced the government to sanction the union, Walesa, by this time a Nobel Peace Prize laureate, was chosen in a free election to be the president of the country that once persecuted him.

For more information:
www.nobelprize.org/peace/laureates/1983/
walesa-bio.html

LIGHTHOUSE KEEPER'S DAUGHTER IN DRAMATIC RESCUE

Grace Darling, twenty-three, daughter of the keeper of the Longstone Lighthouse off England's Northumberland Coast, looked out across a stormy sea one morning in 1838 and spotted a ship aground, almost a mile away. Survivors were clinging to the wreck but her father thought a rescue would be too risky. Grace, however, couldn't idly sit by. She pleaded until her father gave in. Together they headed out in the storm in their rowboat. According to the citation later given to Grace by the Royal Humane Society, "The ocean, lashed by the tempest into the most tumultuous commotion, presented a barrier which would have seemed to all but those two intrepid persons wholly insurmountable by human energy." By the time Grace and her father arrived, nine survivors were hanging on. Grace and her father helped them into the little boat and rowed back through the treacherous waves to the lighthouse. When the story spread, Grace became a national hero.

"*Any man can work when every stroke of his hand brings down the fruit rattling from the tree to the ground; but to labor in season and out of season, under every discouragement, by the power of truth...that requires a heroism which is transcendent.*"

—Henry Ward Beecher, American preacher and writer

CUSTODIAN HERO OF PARKING LOT GUNFIGHT

When Nancy Browning, a church custodian in Pensacola, Florida, heard gunfire in 2002, she ran outside to the parking lot and found an elderly woman bleeding from the hand and another woman waving a revolver. Browning rushed to the wounded woman, Joyce K. Anderson, sixty, and stepped between her and the attacker. "Don't shoot!" Browning yelled as the other woman pulled the trigger. A bullet tore into Browning's abdomen and she fell. In that moment, another man tackled the assailant, holding her until the police arrived. Both women survived, but Browning's heroic actions left her partially paralyzed.

SOLDIER SHIELDS COMRADES FROM GRENADE BLAST

Marine Corporal Jason Dunham was leading a patrol through the town of Karbala, Iraq, in pursuit of insurgents who had ambushed an American convoy in 2004. As Dunham approached a beat-up car, an Iraqi dressed in black leapt out and lunged at him, grabbing the twenty-two-year-old Marine by the throat. Two comrades ran to help and heard Dunham yelling, "No, no, no! Watch his hand!" In the confusing moments that followed, Corporal Dunham broke free from the Iraqi's grip and threw himself headfirst on the ground. Then there was a terrific explosion. No one saw exactly what happened, but Marines examining the scene determined that the Iraqi had activated a grenade and Dunham fell on it, covering it with his Kevlar helmet in hopes that it would absorb the impact. His action saved the two Marines closest to him, but Dunham was seriously wounded and died six days later. Dunham became the first soldier from the war in Iraq to be nominated for the Medal of Honor.

For information on Medals of Honor: www.cmohs.org

IN FIERCE BATTLE, DOG SAVES OWNER FROM GATOR

One evening in 2001, eighty-five-year-old Ruth Gay of LaBelle, Florida, was out for a walk next to a canal with her dog Blue, a two-year-old Australian blue heeler, when she tripped and fell, dislocating her hip. She couldn't move and no one could hear her cries for help—except for a hungry twelve-foot alligator. Suddenly Blue started barking and ran off. Seconds later, Ruth heard hissing, snapping, yelping, and furious barking. Ruth realized that Blue was trying to scare off the monster. The battle went on for several minutes until Blue had driven off the gator. But soon it came back. Once again, the valiant pooch charged into battle, but this time he was repeatedly bitten. When everything fell silent, Ruth thought Blue was dead. But he wasn't. Despite more than two dozen bite wounds, Blue still had the strength to get help and lead family members to Ruth. After Ruth and Blue recovered from their injuries, Blue was honored by Kibbles 'n Bits as the Dog Hero of the Year, the first ever to fight an alligator in the forty-seven-year history of the award.

For more information about the award:
www.delmontedoghero.com/about.asp

FIREFIGHTER CRAWLS THROUGH DEADLY SMOKE FOR GIRL

New York City firefighter Lt. Joseph Clerici pried open the door of the burning apartment in 1995 and thought, "No one can possibly be alive in there." But six-year-old Cindia Rojas was trapped inside, and Clerici couldn't let her die. Crawling on his belly in the few inches of air between the floor and the thick smoke, Clerici reached Cindia's bedroom, where he found her unconscious under her burning bed. Smothering the flames on her clothing and clutching Cindia to his chest, he started inching his way back through the ever-worsening fire. Clerici knew Cindia was probably dead, and he could move faster without her, but he couldn't just leave her. Just as the slim layer of air along the floor vanished, Clerici felt the hands of other firefighters yanking him out of the apartment. As paramedics gave Clerici oxygen, he learned to his joy that his effort had not been in vain. Cindia was alive. Although badly burned, she would eventually return home.

You can read more firefighter stories in *The Greatest Firefighter Stories Never Told* by Michael Santangelo, Mara Bovsun, and Allan Zullo (Andrews McMeel Publishing, 2002).

RAILMEN RIDE EXPLOSIVE EXPRESS OUT OF TOWN

Railroad engineers James Nightall and Ben Gimbert were hauling a dangerous cargo—forty freight cars filled with two-hundred-fifty-pound and five-hundred-pound bombs—through the town of Soham, Cambs, England, in 1944. As the train neared the town, Gimbert noticed flames rising from one of the front freight cars. He stopped the engine and, with Nightall, unhitched all the cars behind the burning car. Then at full throttle, the two engineers hauled the burning explosives toward open country. Tragically, they didn't make it. The burning car blew up, damaging several hundred homes. Nightall was killed and Gimbert seriously injured, but their courageous act saved the town. Had they not tried their desperate getaway, the whole train would have blown up, taking the town of Soham with it.

"Courage is doing what you're afraid to do. There can be no courage unless you're scared."

—Eddie Rickenbacker, World War I flying ace

HOMEMAKER SAVES GIRL
FROM COUGAR

While Myra Baloun, a forty-three-year-old home-maker, was camping near Hope, British Columbia, in 1999, she heard screaming coming from the woods. Seven-year-old Tayla Westgard and two other girls had been playing at a nearby campsite when a cougar attacked her. The other girls fled. Baloun ran toward Tayla and shouted at the cougar, who had part of the girl's torso in his mouth. Picking up a thick branch, Baloun struck the animal several times until it released Tayla. Baloun pulled the bleeding girl to her feet and then fled the scene with her. Tracked down by authorities, the cougar was found in a tree about two hundred feet away and was destroyed. Tayla was hospitalized for a severe eye injury and numerous lacerations, but she recovered.

For more information: www.carnegiehero.org

MAILMAN DELIVERS TWO FROM DROWNING

In 2003, a small truck had lost its brakes in heavy traffic and skidded into a lake in Germantown, Tennessee, and started sinking. Trapped inside were Robert Byington, a dialysis patient, and his wife, Betty. Mailman Rodger Parker saw the accident and, leaving his car in traffic, charged down to the lake and dove in. Robert rolled down the window just as Parker arrived. The mailman easily pulled Betty out, but Robert was stuck. Even though two other rescuers had come to help, they couldn't extricate him from the car. Parker, an old Navy man, was not about to let him go down. As the truck was sinking and pulling Parker underwater, he reached in the window, trying to free Robert. Just as the truck hit the bottom, he yanked the man free, saving his life. "The greatest angels on earth are the heroes," said Betty at a ceremony in Washington, D.C., where Parker was lauded as the National Association of Letter Carriers' 2003 Hero of the Year. "And Mr. Parker is a hero."

For more information: www.nalc.org/commun/heroes

COWS FORM CIRCLE OF
LIFE AROUND FARMER

In 1996, farmer Donald Mottram, of Medirim, Wales, was zipping across his property on a motorbike when an angry bull slammed into him, sending him flying. Mottram landed on his back and was staring up into the eyes of the enraged bull. The thirty-three-hundred-pound beast started stomping on Mottram. *I'm going to die*, the farmer thought before he passed out. But he didn't count on an old friend—Daisy, his favorite cow. When he came to, he was surrounded by a large group of cows, led by Daisy, that crowded around him, keeping the bull at bay. Each time the angry bull charged, the cows would block him. Daisy kept the cows in formation, protecting Mottram until he managed to crawl to safety. He was seriously hurt, but thanks to Daisy, he survived the terrifying attack.

MILL BOSS HERO AFTER DEVASTATING FIRE

In 1995, Aaron Feuerstein was enjoying his seventieth birthday party at a Boston restaurant, unaware that a few miles away, his life was going up in smoke. A boiler had exploded at the fabric mill he owned and now the business, which his father had founded nine decades earlier, was reduced to scorched rubble. Many of his thirty-two-hundred workers expected Feuerstein to close up, leaving them jobless. But the old-style businessman surprised them. Instead of cutting his losses, Feuerstein, rebuilt the plant and paid salaries and benefits—at a cost of $1.5 million a week—to his employees while they were waiting for the factory to crank up again. Within a month, the majority of his workers were back at their jobs. His actions made Feuerstein a hero, even though it may have seemed insane in today's brutal dog-eat-dog business world. But Feuerstein didn't care. "In a place where there's moral depravity and no feeling of moral responsibility," he told *People* magazine, "do your damnedest to be a man."

SUBWAY RIDER
COLLARS SLASHER

Anthony Gallo heard screams as the subway he was waiting for lumbered into a station in Brooklyn in July 2003. A deranged man had just slashed rider Erica Paul, forty-six, in the face and was bolting toward the doors of the train as they slid open. Gallo, a thirty-nine-year-old alarm installer from Astoria, wasn't about to let him get away. He followed the slasher, twenty-three-year-old Dave Smith, and tackled him. While Gallo tried to hold him to the ground, Smith put up a mighty struggle, slashing his captor in the wrist. But the muscular Gallo held on tight until police arrived and arrested Smith, a homeless man wanted for a similar attack. "This guy was crazy," Gallo later told the *New York Post*. "He was carrying a bag filled with steak knives." After the attack, Gallo received an NYPD citation. "Mr. Gallo is a true New York hero," said Police Commissioner Ray Kelly. Said Gallo, "I just did what I had to do. Who knows what could have happened if this guy got away. He could have killed someone."

> *"I just do whatever it is that I believe I should do, regardless of the risks to my life."*

—Corazon Aquino, president of the Philippines

NEIGHBOR RESCUES INFANT FROM BLAZING HOUSE

Sean Christopher Hough sprang into action after learning a one-year-old boy was trapped on the second floor of a neighbor's burning house in McHenry, Illinois, in 2003. To get past the flames on the first floor, Hough, a thirty-one-year-old teacher, mounted the railing on a deck, then grabbed a ladder to reach the window where the child was sleeping in his crib. With his T-shirt over his face to filter the smoke, Hough felt along the walls, then found the crib and snatched the baby. Hough dropped the child to the waiting arms of people below and then climbed down. Both the child and his rescuer were treated for smoke inhalation and recovered.

FIVE-YEAR-OLD CHASES CROOK FROM HOME

A five-year-old boy turned crime fighter when he chased a burglar from his family's home in Bradley Stoke, Bristol, England. "What are you doing?" asked little Nicholas White when he confronted a spike-haired stranger who was taking a wallet off the dining room table in 2004. "That's not yours, so put it back," the child demanded. Then Nicholas chased the thief through the dining room, kitchen, and out into the garden. "I told him to put it back and he ran for it," Nicholas said later. "My parents think I'm really brave, but I wasn't at all scared." The thief got away with the wallet, but Nicholas's brave act kept the thief from stealing a purse with over two hundred dollars in cash inside.

GERMAN SHEPHERD HERO TWICE OVER

Kaiser, a big German shepherd who lived in the back room of Angelo Fiocchi's candy store in lower Manhattan, was a hero twice in 1926. One summer night, he sniffed trouble in Fiocchi's shop. He trotted into the front room and found two men with blackjacks about to whack his master over the head. Snarling and flashing teeth, Kaiser went after the assailants and drove them to the street. A few months later, Kaiser and Fiocchi's friend John Coda were playing along the Hudson River. Coda threw a stick into the water for Kaiser to retrieve, then fell in himself, and slipped under the surface because he couldn't swim. Kaiser swam to where he saw bubbles and when Coda surfaced again, the dog grabbed him by the shirt collar and kept him afloat until rescuers could pull the pair out with a boat hook.

TEEN BREAKS SUV WINDOW, SAVES DROWNING WOMAN

Shameeza Ishahak's SUV veered off the road and plunged into a canal near Cooper City, Florida, in 2002. The vehicle was sinking fast in fifteen feet of water and she couldn't swim. Suddenly, she heard banging on the window of the front passenger door. It was Daniel Lennon, an eighteen-year-old high school student. He had been riding in a car passing nearby at the time of Ishahak's accident. Without hesitation, he had stripped off his clothes and swam to the vehicle, which was sinking nose-down in the water. With his fist, Lennon banged on the window until it broke, then reached in, and dragged Ishahak out of the SUV. Fighting for breath, he pulled her to the surface and swam her to the nearest bank and safety.

HEROES FROM HISTORY
The Little Rock Nine

They were just a bunch of high school kids, ready for their first day of classes. Then they walked up to the front door of Central High School in Little Rock, Arkansas, kicking open the door to equal education for black students all over America. *Brown vs. the Board of Education* had outlawed school segregation, but intimidation and threats had scared black students away. Then these nine teenagers stepped across the threshold of one of the most notoriously racist schools in the country. On their first day of school, the group was met by an angry mob. "I looked into the face of an old woman, and it seemed a kind face, but when I looked at her again, she spat at me," recalled one of the students, Elizabeth Eckford, who was fifteen at the time. Despite death threats and constant harassment, the nine kids stood their ground. Several graduated from Central, and all went on to successful lives.

For more information: www.centralhigh57.org

COMRADE USES AX
TO BREAK DEADLY
BEAR HUG

Forest firefighter Konrad Nygaard, twenty, and his colleague Ian Matheson, thirty, made camp in the woods of Alberta, Canada, after battling a blaze in 1994, hoping to relax for the night. But they were soon hoping just to survive the night. A large black bear attacked Matheson, snapping its huge jaws on his back. Nygaard grabbed an ax, swung it, but missed. The bear grasped Matheson in his claws and bit him harder. Nygaard swung again, this time hitting the bear square in the back. The bruin dropped its prey and hobbled off, leaving the men to call for help. A helicopter lifted the men to base camp. From there, Matheson was taken to a hospital, where he was treated for several puncture wounds and recovered. Nygaard won a Carnegie Hero's award for fighting off the bear.

For more information: www.carnegiehero.org

DRIVER PINS JUMPER
TO BRIDGE

Rajon Barin Begin, twenty-seven, was driving over a bridge in Fremont, California, in 1994 when he spotted a young man standing on the parapet, clinging to a chain link fence, about to jump forty-five feet to the railroad tracks below. Begin stopped his car, walked over to the twenty-year-old man and tried to convince the would-be jumper to come down, but it was clear the man was not listening. So Begin walked out onto the four-inch-wide parapet and slowly made his way for seventy feet to the jumper. Then, he straddled the man, grabbing the chain links and using his own body to pin him to the fence. The man outweighed him and struggled to shake his captor off, but Begin stood firm, keeping the man pressed against the fence until police and firefighters arrived. They convinced the jumper to allow them to pull him to safety. It wasn't until later that Begin realized he had been clutching the chain links so hard he bruised his hands.

CAT BECOMES
WAR HERO

During the battle of Stalingrad in 1942, a stray cat named Mourka did more than boost morale of the Russian troops. He served as a "runner," bringing vital messages from the forward gun positions back to the commander at headquarters when fighting was too fierce for human soldiers to get through. Mourka performed his mission courageously for several months before, sadly, he was declared missing in action.

RETIREE MAKES LIFESAVING LEAP INTO FLAMES

Clay T. Jones, forty-two, was unconscious, trapped upside down in his car after he slammed into a utility pole and turned over in Sumter, South Carolina, in July 2002. Despite gasoline spilling from the car and flames licking the rear of the vehicle, Richard H. Spencer Jr., a forty-five-year-old retired firefighter, first tried to snuff out the blaze with a fire extinguisher. When that didn't work, Spencer had no choice but to brave the flames and enter the burning car. He opened the driver's door, crawled in, freed Jones, and dragged him to safety. The fact that Spencer suffered from heart disease didn't stop him from attempting this daring and strenuous rescue, which saved a life.

ICE CREAM ACTIVIST
RIDES TO RESCUE

Maria Campanella, the "Ice Cream Lady" of Bensonhurst, Brooklyn, delivers a lot more than sweet treats from her truck. She also brings hope and charity. The middle-aged rolling philanthropist brings toys to needy kids at the Marlboro Housing Projects, hands out yellow ribbons to support Mothers Against Drunk Driving, and helps organize meetings for the American Red Cross. Her truck sometimes carries potted plants for a public garden she created on the Belt Parkway as part of the Adopt-a-Highway program. Once, she even saved a life. An old man collapsed on the sidewalk in front of her, and she leapt out and performed CPR. "All the stuff I do behind this ice-cream truck, you wouldn't believe," she told the *New York Post*, which awarded her a Liberty Medal in 2004.

For more information: www.nypost.com/libertymedals

"It's true that heroes are inspiring, but mustn't they also do some rescuing if they are to be worthy of their name? Would Wonder Woman matter if she only sent commiserating telegrams to the distressed?"

—Jeanette Winterson, writer

TEENS FREE ELDERLY MAN SINKING IN MUD

Three school chums from Hamworthy, England, were boating when they spotted an old man flailing about in the mud. An eighty-eight-year-old retired toolmaker had wandered away from home, gotten lost, and stumbled into the mudflats, where he started to sink. He had been stuck for about six hours when the boys—Sam Shiner, Matthew Pepper, and Noel Creche, all thirteen—spotted him waving his arms frantically. "We were all frightened because we were sinking as well," Noel told BBC News later. Eight attempts to pull him out failed. Then Sam suggested taking off the man's trousers to slide him out. That was when he came free. It took the boys an hour and a half, but they said that they would do it again.

CHILD'S CHAT KEEPS MOM FROM DYING IN PLANE WRECK

First there was a loud boom, then blinding light filled the cabin when Japan Airlines Flight 123 slammed into a mountain and burst into flames in August 1985, killing all but four of the five hundred twenty-four people aboard the Boeing 747 jumbo jet. One more life might have been lost had it not been for the courage of one small girl—eight-year-old Mikko Yoshiaki. The girl's mother, Hiroko, thirty-five, had been injured and was lapsing into unconsciousness. Rather than free herself, Mikko called out, "Don't go to sleep, mother. Stay awake or you'll die." Mikko kept talking to her mother, keeping Hiroko awake for an excruciating sixteen hours before rescuers reached them and lifted them to safety.

LIONHEARTED POOCH PROTECTS KIDS FROM RATTLER

Leo, a three-year-old white standard poodle, showed lionhearted courage by battling a giant rattlesnake in 1984. Sean Callahan, eleven, and his sister Erin, nine, were playing in a creek on their parents' ranch in Hunt, Texas, when the boy tripped over a five-and-a-half-foot diamondback rattler that had been dozing in the roots of a cypress tree. Just as the snake attacked, Leo lunged at it, allowing Sean to escape. But the brave pooch took six bites from the poisonous reptile before Sean's mother, Lana, killed the snake with a rifle. Leo was rushed to the vet. The dog's face was so swollen that the vet couldn't even find his left eye and doubted the dog would survive. Leo lingered between life and death for three days, but in time he recovered. The vet believed Leo beat the odds only because he had a remarkable will to live.

RACE FAN SAVES SPECTATOR FROM FLYING DEBRIS

Erik Raymond, an eighteen-year-old cook, was in the stands enjoying a stock-car race at Pinellas Park, Florida, in 1980. Suddenly, two cars slammed into each other on the race track. To his horror, a wheel flew off an axle, bounced over the barrier, and was flying straight toward Donna Sue Altiere, thirty-two, who was sitting next to him. As spectators scattered, Raymond, covered her body with his. The wheel struck Raymond, knocking him unconscious. Mrs. Altiere was not injured. Raymond recovered following hospitalization.

WOMAN RESCUES BOY
CLINGING TO SIDE
OF BLUFF

Jean Burgmeier, thirty-nine, an elementary-school principal in Dubuque, Iowa, was riding her bicycle in 2000 along a wooded bluff that overlooked the Mississippi River when she encountered a frantic boy who told her his friend, seven-year-old Jeffery Kraft, was in terrible danger. The two boys had been playing on the bluff when Jeffery tumbled down a steep slope. He stopped his fall by grasping rocks and earth just short of the edge of the bluff and was now clinging to the side, only a few feet from a potential death plunge. Burgmeier raced to the scene. Carefully, she wedged herself into a rock formation, then reached down and grabbed Jeffery by the hand. She secured him for several minutes until rescue personnel arrived. Forming a human chain, firefighters reached the two, then passed Jeffery to the top of the slope and helped Burgmeier up. Jeffery was treated at a hospital for cuts and bruises.

For more information: www.carnegiehero.org

"Few men are willing to brave the disapproval of their fellows, the censure of their colleagues, the wrath of their society. Moral courage is a rarer commodity than bravery in battle or great intelligence. Yet it is the one essential, vital quality for those who seek to change a world which yields most painfully to change."

—Robert F. Kennedy, U.S. Attorney General and New York senator

DREDGE OPERATOR PULLS DROWNING BOY FROM RIVER

Recent rains had left the waters of the Baker River near Warren, New Hampshire, cold and turbulent in August 2003. Christopher Oikle, a twenty-one-year-old dredge operator, knew the conditions were too dangerous for swimming, but that didn't stop him when it was a matter of life or death. Not realizing the hazard, Jared Champigny, thirteen, had jumped from a boulder into a swirling whirlpool and was being pulled under the water. Alerted by the screams of Jared's family, Oikle dove into the raging river, swam to the struggling boy, and grabbed him around the chest. Then he tied Jared to a line that others on the riverbank had dropped from the top of the boulder. After they pulled Jared out, they tossed the line back for Oikle and hauled him back to dry land.

WHISTLEBLOWER RIPS BIG TOBACCO'S SMOKE SCREEN

Biochemist Jeffrey Wigand was hired by the tobacco company Brown & Williamson to develop a nonaddictive cigarette. But he soon discovered that the tobacco industry had a hidden agenda to hook young smokers. In 1993, five years after he left the company, Wigand told the world what tobacco companies didn't want anyone to hear. The information he gave government investigators, lawyers, and reporters led to a multibillion-dollar settlement in which the industry was ordered to pay tobacco-related medical expenses. For blowing the whistle, Wigand endured harassment and death threats. His marriage dissolved and he left the industry. But he rose from the ashes to become a teacher and establish a nonprofit organization—Smoke-Free Kids—to warn children about the dangers of that first puff.

For more information: www.jeffreywigand.com

DOG BRINGS WATER TO INJURED FARMER

While Herbert Jones was pruning the trees in his Umatilla, Florida, pecan grove in May 1953, he tumbled from his ladder and broke his back. Luckily for him, he had a faithful companion with him—Cocoa, his little brown dog. Unable to move, Jones was dying of thirst. "Water, Cocoa," he repeated to the dog. Eventually Cocoa got the message and ran to a water pail in the house where Jones lived alone. Cocoa returned carrying drops of water on his tongue for his master to lick off. This went on for five days until a visitor found Jones and brought him to the hospital. "Cocoa saved my life," Jones said.

RESTAURANT PATRON THWARTS KNIFEMAN

In the dead of night in 2002, a crook with a knife entered a Vancouver, Washington, restaurant and grabbed manager Anthony P. Jensen. "Do what I say or I'll kill you," he snarled as he held the knife to the throat of the terrified twenty-three-year-old. However, one of the three patrons at the late night eatery, trucker Jonathan H. Bolender, fifty, refused to stand by. Bolender jumped on the attacker who began slashing at him. Before he could get the knife away and wrestle the assailant, Bolender suffered ten stab wounds to his back and thighs. Nevertheless, he pinned the attacker until police arrived. Thanks to Bolender's quick action and determination, Jensen escaped with minor injuries. Bolender, whose wounds were serious, recovered after a lengthy hospital stay.

CANCER GIRL'S LEMONADE RAISES RESEARCH DOLLARS

As a toddler, Alexandra Scott was handed a lemon. Before her first birthday, doctors in Philadelphia found a cancerous tumor on her spine, paralyzing her from the chest down. But at age three, the plucky little girl told her parents that she was ready to go into business with a lemonade stand. But this would have a twist—all the money would go to cancer research. At first, her mother, Liz, was worried that her daughter might be disappointed. "I warned her it would be hard to make a difference selling lemonade at fifty cents a cup," she said. In her first year, the frail child raised two thousand dollars. More money poured in, then other people and corporations got involved. Alex set a goal of a million dollars. The goal was reached in 2004, but sadly she did not live to see it, dying three months earlier at age seven. Before she died, she told her brother her new goal was five million dollars. Her family has vowed to work "like Alex" to make it happen.

For more information: www.alexslemonade.com

DOORMAN TURNS HERO
IN BLACKOUT

When the massive multistate power failure plunged much of the country into darkness on August 14, 2003, Elizabeth Bethune, eighty-three, was stranded in the lobby of the Jeffersonian Apartments senior complex in Detroit, too frail to climb the seventeen stories to her home. After several hours, the building's twenty-eight-year-old doorman David Evans realized it might take all night for the power to return, too long for Bethune to survive sitting in the lobby. Evans carefully draped the woman across his shoulders and carried her up all seventeen flights. The same day, Evans also summoned emergency medical help and hauled some of the equipment up twenty-two flights for a sick resident. For his blackout heroics, Evans was awarded a Red Cross Everyday Hero award.

For information about other recipients:
www.redcross.org/services/hss/newspro/
heroarchive.html

NURSE TRIO KEEPS PREEMIE ALIVE WHEN POWER DIES

At just a little over three pounds, the eleven-week-old premature baby at the intensive care neonatal unit in New York's Bellevue Hospital Center needed an electric ventilator to breathe. When the 2003 multistate blackout occurred, the nurses in the unit didn't worry because the hospital had its own generator. Then that failed. "Suddenly all the ventilator alarms went off and it became dark," recalled Thelma Faderan, a nurse practitioner on duty that night. A team of three nurses worked together to keep the baby, born fifteen weeks early, alive. Anat Gross used her hand to pump the ventilator so the baby could breathe, while Zenaida Banzon held a light, and Faderan monitored vital signs until the generator came back on in half an hour. Later, the three were among twenty-nine people honored by the city. Mayor Bloomberg said they "helped save one of the smallest New Yorkers."

HERO FROM HISTORY
Abraham Lincoln

Born in a log cabin on February 12, 1809, Abraham Lincoln would one day be judged by many historians as America's greatest president. A lawyer who was defeated after one term in Congress, Lincoln was losing interest in politics. But when the passage of the Kansas-Nebraska Act opened more parts of the Union to slavery in 1854, Lincoln, who viewed slavery as immoral, charged back into the political arena. "As I would not be a slave, so I would not be a master. This expresses my idea of democracy," he wrote in 1859. A year later "Honest Abe" was the leader of a warring nation. Among the drastic—and some believed dictatorial—measures he took to save the country was the Emancipation Proclamation, abolishing slavery. Five days after the Civil War ended, an assassin shot and killed Lincoln during a performance of "Our American Cousin" at Ford's Theater in Washington, D.C.

RAPPELLING COP SAVES DANGLING WORKER

I t sounded like an explosion when a cable snapped on a scaffold, leaving brick workers Roberto Hernandez and Jose Lopez dangling twelve stories over the pavement in New York City in 1999. Hernandez was easily rescued with a fire ladder, but Lopez was disoriented and hanging by a rope. Police Officer Romano Amleto knew he didn't have time to spare. In a daring move, he rappelled down the side of the building and hitched the worker's safety harness to his own. It was a tremendous risk, because no one knew whether the rope could hold the weight of two men. Amleto carefully lowered them to the street below, where a crowd of two hundred broke into wild cheers.

Suggested reading:
What Cops Know by Connie Fletcher
(Pocket Books, 1992)

PASSERBY RESCUES TRUCKER IN CAB DANGLING OVER BRIDGE

A tractor-trailer driven by James Dawson, thirty-nine, broke through a bridge railing in Seattle in 1978, leaving him trapped in the cab, which was tilted on its side and hanging fifty-five feet above Lake Washington by only one of its hinges and two of its brake air hoses. To make matters worse, the engine was on fire. Other motorists put out the fire with an extinguisher. Despite the threat that the cab would plunge into the water, passerby Erin Dan Carew, twenty-three, was determined to save Dawson. Carew inched his way to the cab by walking along the upturned side of the rig. When he reached the cab, it began to teeter on the edge of the bridge. Kneeling on the flipped side of the cab, Carew pried open the driver's door and helped Dawson climb out. Both men then carefully made it to safety. For his bravery, Carew earned a Carnegie Hero award.

For more information: carnegiehero.org

"Cautious, careful people, always casting about to preserve their reputation and social standing, never can bring about a reform. Those who are really in earnest must be willing to be anything or nothing in the world's estimation, and publicly and privately, in season and out, avow their sympathy with despised and persecuted ideas and their advocates, and bear the consequences."

—Susan B. Anthony, suffragist

CAT SCRATCH WARNS PAIR
OF ERUPTING VOLCANO

Toto the cat lived with an elderly couple, Gianni and Irma, in a house in the shadow of Mount Vesuvius. One night in 1944, the agitated kitty started pouncing on his sleeping masters, finally scratching Gianni's face. The old man chased Toto around the room. But Irma insisted that the cat's weird actions were a sign to flee. It was a good thing. Shortly after the couple hit the road, the volcano erupted. The molten lava that buried their house would have killed them had Toto not sounded the warning meow.

BAYWATCH STAR IN
REAL LIFE RESCUE

When *Baywatch* hunk David Hasselhoff witnessed an auto accident in Los Angeles in 1995, he proved that he was more than a pretty face and a set of impressive pecs and washboard abs. He helped save an unconscious car crash victim by moving her head to clear her airway. By the time the ambulance arrived, the actor had the woman stabilized, reported *People* magazine. The emergency medical service technicians were impressed, even though they didn't recognize the famous TV life-guard. "Are you a paramedic?" one asked. "No," Hasselhoff replied, "but I play one on TV."

WITH ROTTWEILER
AT BAT,
CROOKS STRIKE OUT

Trucker Herb Blish learned the importance of having a pal who goes to bat for you after three thugs tried to hold him up on an interstate near Walcott, Iowa, in 1995. Blish was about to leave a truck stop when two young men approached him and demanded money. He refused, unaware that a third man, holding a baseball bat, was hiding behind the front end of the rig. Lucky for Blish, the bandit couldn't hide from the trucker's traveling partner, a ninety-three-pound Rottweiler named Mariah. She had been lounging on the front seat of the cab. When she saw Blish in trouble, she leapt through the window. Although she tore ligaments in her leg from jumping seven feet to the ground, she attacked and disarmed the bat-wielding man. Then Mariah, with the large end of the bat in her sharp teeth, ran toward the two other crooks. The sight of the big dog carrying the bat sent the roadside bandits fleeing for their lives.

PASSERBY WADES THROUGH GASOLINE TO HELP INJURED TRUCKER

Chris A. Cole had to splash through gasoline to save a trucker whose tractor-trailer, which was carrying seven thousand gallons of the flammable fuel, overturned in 2002 near Bradford, Pennsylvania. Driver Michael G. Bradley, thirty-six, had been making a turn when the truck tipped over on its right side. Bradley pushed his battered body halfway out the window on the driver's side, but was too seriously injured to free himself. Cole, passing by in his car when the accident happened, saw the gallons of gasoline gushing out of the tank and knew that Cole was in a desperate situation. The truck's engine was still running and it could spark an inferno at any second. Cole dashed through the gasoline to the cab and pulled Bradley to safety. By the time he got there, he was covered with flammable liquid. Fortunately, the engine stopped running on its own, avoiding a major explosion. Both men were treated at the hospital and released.

For more information: www.carnegiehero.org

TUG'S CREW SAVES ONE HUNDRED FIFTY-FIVE FROM BURNING SHIP

A 1904 excursion on the steamship General Slocum turned to terror for thirteen hundred passengers on their way to Long Island when the ship became a floating bonfire. Many nearby boat owners figured efforts to help would be both dangerous and futile. But not Jack Wade, captain of the tugboat John Wade, named in honor of his father. At full throttle, he reached the blazing ship. Heat from the fire blistered the paint and shattered the windows of his tug, but Wade refused to turn back. "You'll lose your tug and livelihood," his pilot warned. Wade shouted back, "Damn the tug!" With his boat bumping against the burning steamship, desperate mothers dropped their babies over the side to the waiting arms of Wade and his crewmembers. Other passengers jumped onto his deck. Meanwhile, members of his six-man crew leapt overboard and rescued dozens of passengers who had jumped into the water and were drowning. The death toll from the General Slocum fire was 1,021. But it would have been significantly higher without Captain Wade and his crew, who rescued 155 people.

You can read more about the Slocum disaster in
Ship Ablaze: The Tragedy of the Steamship General Slocum by
Edward T. O'Donnell (Broadway, 2003).

"To go against the dominant thinking of your friends, of most of the people you see every day, is perhaps the most difficult act of heroism you can perform."

—Theodore H. White, author

DOUGHBOY MAKES MINCEMEAT OF NO-MAN'S-LAND FOE

Machine-gun bullets were whizzing all around them, coming from a line of German trenches in No-Man's-Land in 1918. Dozens of doughboys in Pvt. Michael Valente's company lay dead or wounded. The twenty-three-year-old Italian immigrant, who had settled in New York City a short time before the war, couldn't take it anymore. Valente flew into a rage and rushed directly toward the enemy trenches, firing his rifle until he ran out of bullets. Then he stormed more of the machine gun nests, jumping from trench to trench, tossing in hand grenades. A wound to his arm only made him madder. Close behind Valente was another soldier, Pvt. Joseph Mastine, a bartender and cigar maker from upstate New York, who sprayed the Germans with gunfire. By the time Valente calmed down, he had wiped out four machine gun nests, captured twenty prisoners, and sent the rest of the German troops running for their lives. Valente's outburst saved his company and earned him the Medal of Honor. His sidekick Mastine got a Distinguished Service Cross as well as a cigar named after him.

For information on Medals of Honor: www.cmohs.org

DISABLED DAD STANDS
UP TO NEIGHBOR
FROM HELL

Richard Lloyd was the neighbor from hell. The unemployed forty-three-year-old bully had already driven one family from the house next door in the Conwy village of Dwygyfylchi, Wales, through constant threats and intimidation. When Noel Kennerley, thirty-three, and his family moved in next door in 2003, Lloyd started harassing them right away. The abuse was relentless and the Kennerleys were not alone. Lloyd had threatened almost everyone in the village. Instead of packing up and moving, Kennerley, who was disabled from a car accident, fought back through the courts. He campaigned for an antisocial behavior order and won it. The order kicked Lloyd out of town and barred him from ever entering it again. For having the guts to stand up to the bully, Kennerley was given a reward of one thousand pounds, which he donated to charity. "I was adamant I wasn't going to take it," said Kennerley, "and that infuriated him all the more, which made him more aggressive and determined, which ultimately led to his downfall."

INJURED NAVY CAT
STAYS ON JOB

Simon, a black and white tomcat, was the pet of Lt. Commander I. R. Griffiths, captain of the British frigate *Amethyst*, in Hong Kong. When the Red Chinese swept across the mainland in 1949, the *Amethyst* was sent to Nanking, where it was attacked en route. Commander Griffiths was killed and Simon was injured and badly burned. But despite his injuries, he still did his duty, catching and killing rats. The cat's courage made headlines in England, and he was a hailed as a hero. Sadly, three weeks after the *Amethyst* reached safe port, Simon died. He was posthumously awarded a medal for bravery.

TOT IS CATCH OF THE
DAY FOR DINER

Larry Abeyta, fifty-one, was dining with his girlfriend at Old Tony's, a seaside restaurant in Redondo Beach, California, in 2003. All of a sudden, a three-year-old girl in the restaurant tumbled out a large open window into the ocean. "Help her!" the girl's mother screamed. Abeyta leapt through the same window, jumping twenty feet into the ocean below. He quickly found the girl, who was floating face down, and grabbed her. Fortunately, she began breathing again. Holding her, Abeyta swam to the restaurant's pier and delivered her to her parents. Officials said she would have died if Abeyta had not acted swiftly. After the dramatic rescue, Abeyta sat down soaking wet and dove into his halibut and shrimp entrée. His girlfriend suggested they leave, but Abeyta would not hear of it. "We came here to have dinner, so let's have dinner," he said.

NEIGHBOR SAVES WOMAN FROM ATTACKER

Dennis Schroeder was in his Midland, Michigan, home in 2003 when he heard a woman screaming for help from the upper floor of the apartment building. He rushed upstairs to the apartment where the cries were coming from, but the door was locked. Schroeder kicked the door in and discovered a man standing over the screaming woman, hitting her with a hammer. Grabbing the nearest heavy object, a large floor fan, Schroeder stepped between the woman and her attacker. He held the fan up for protection and talked the man into dropping the hammer. Midland police said that thanks to Schroeder's quick action and courage, the woman escaped with just a few injuries to her head and arm. Without him, authorities believe she might have been seriously hurt or killed.

"The credit belongs to the man who is actually in the arena, whose face is marred by dust and sweat and blood, who strives valiantly, who errs and comes short again and again, who knows the great enthusiasms, the great devotions, and spends himself in a worthy cause, who at best knows achievement and who at the worst if he fails at least fails while daring greatly so that his place shall never be with those cold and timid souls who know neither victory nor defeat."

—President Theodore Roosevelt

CLERK DESCENDS INTO FIRE PIT TO WARN MINER

When fire broke out in Utah's Clear Creek mine in 1899, one miner was left inside, working too deep to hear the explosions and frantic warning shouts that sent his comrades fleeing. Several men tried to get him, but were driven back by the flames. Turning off the fan that blew air into the mine would contain the fire, but that would mean the death of the lone miner. The foreman asked for volunteers to try another rescue attempt. None of the experienced miners stepped forward. But then Heber Franklin, a young office worker who had never set foot in that dangerous subterranean world, shouted, "I'll go!" Franklin and the foreman dashed past the flames and found the miner deep in the tunnel still at work. The three rushed to safety before the fan was shut off, snuffing the flames. Authorities were impressed with the young clerk's courage. "He was the only man of the many standing by whose nerve did not desert him," noted the *New York Times*.

TEEN HELPS OTHERS TO SAFETY IN TERRORIST SIEGE

Student Soslan Gusiev, sixteen, had given up hope of surviving as the terrorist siege of his school in Beslan, Russia, wore on through its second day in 2004. He wrote his name on his leg so his family could identify his body. But when the thirty-two terrorists started exploding bombs, Soslan burst into action. He pushed his twelve-year-old brother, David, out a window. Then instead of leaping to safety himself, he turned back to help eight other children escape. "After I saved my brother, I really didn't care about my own life," he told reporters later. "I was so relieved that my brother was alive that I didn't think of myself. And then I just helped other kids." Russian authorities stormed the school, killing thirty terrorists. Hailed as the hero of Beslan, Gusiev suffers from nightmares from the attack, which killed three hundred thirty-five of the twelve hundred hostages, including teachers, schoolmates, and parents.

RESCUED DOG SAVES FAMILY FROM FLOOD

The Gfoerer family of Cathedral City, California, rescued a starving German shepherd from an abusive owner who wanted to kill his pet. They named the dog Last Chance. Two years later, in 1977, their pet returned the favor, saving the family from a deadly flood. In the middle of the night, Last Chance barked wildly and broke down the door where Clem and Pat Gfoerer were sleeping. When Clem stood up, he was knee-deep in mud and water. Torrential rains had swollen the river near their home. Pat ran to wake their son Billy, seventeen, and everyone ran to the rear of the house, but forty seconds later, a huge wave slammed into them. The family tried to hang from the rafters as wave after wave hit the house until they were all washed through a broken window. The flood carried them thirty yards away until they hit high ground. Everyone, including Last Chance, survived. A Red Cross spokesman said that if the Gfoerers had remained asleep when the waves hit, they all would have died.

DOCTOR SPENDS RETIREMENT HELPING POOR

During a 1981 trip to Delhi, India, German physician Johannes Asmus saw something that disturbed him deeply—scabies-ridden homeless people in agony. He bought some medicine and started tending to them. Suspicious Indian authorities arrested him on charges of being a pedophile or drug dealer, but when they couldn't substantiate any of the accusations, they set Asmus free and he returned to Germany. But he couldn't forget what he had seen. In 1985, he returned to India and recruited volunteers from among the natives and tourists, raising funds to buy medicine to treat the beggars and leprosy victims. At an age when he could be enjoying a comfortable retirement, Asmus works tirelessly among the sick and forgotten of the Connaught neighborhood in India, where, thanks largely to his efforts, the majority of street urchins and homeless are free of illness. When asked why he does it, he said, "I'm a simple man who loves India and wants to help the poor."

MOTORISTS PLUCK
TRUCKER FROM
GATOR SWAMP

Trucker Robert Fordham was in deep trouble after his rig jackknifed in a rainstorm and plunged off a forty-foot bridge into Louisiana's Atchafalaya Swamp in 1988. The two-hundred-seventy-four-pound trucker suffered serious injuries to his back, hip, and head and could barely keep his face above water. But two motorists on the bridge had seen the accident and weren't about to just stand there. William Kessler of Houston and Fred Lalumandier of Bryan, Texas, leapt from the bridge into the water below. Together they helped Fordham out of the cab and towed him to a steep bank, where they waited for an hour until help arrived. Kessler said that as he leapt, he worried about slamming into underwater stumps and not having the strength to help the beefy trucker. It was only later that he realized how big a risk he had taken. The Atchafalaya Swamp is infested with alligators.

For more information: www.carnegiehero.org

"*If we take the generally accepted definition of bravery as a quality which knows no fear, I have never seen a brave man. All men are frightened. The more intelligent they are, the more they are frightened.*"

—George S. Patton, American army general

"LET'S ROLL"

"Are you guys ready? Let's roll." With those words, a young father and software executive became a hero in the war against terror on September 11, 2001. Todd Beamer, thirty-two, was on United Airlines Flight 93 when Al Qaeda hijackers attempted to take over the plane and turn it into a killing machine. Their fellow terrorists had already succeeded in attacking the World Trade Center and the Pentagon. Using his cell phone, Beamer connected with a GTE operator and told her that three hijackers, one with what looked like a bomb on his belt, had commandeered the plane. At the end of the conversation, Beamer said he and the other passengers had decided to try to jump the terrorists. The operator could hear Beamer as he uttered his now-famous battle cry. Cockpit tapes recorded a ferocious struggle as the passengers stood up to the terrorists and thwarted their evil plans. Instead of crashing into a building and killing thousands, the plane went down in a remote field in western Pennsylvania.

FIREMEN'S RESCUE
OF WOMAN
SAVES THEIR LIVES

New York City Fire Department Captain Jay Jonas and his squad of seven were rushing down the stairs of the North Tower of the World Trade Center, which was about to collapse in the 2001 terrorist attacks. At the twentieth floor they came upon Josephine Harris, who was struggling down the stairs. There was no way she could make it on her own so, on his orders, they began carrying her. Jonas figured that he had just signed their death warrants—they were now moving too slowly to get out before the building came down. At the fourth floor, the building started to collapse. "Damn," Jonas said, "we didn't make it." But he was wrong. Behind and in front of them, the stairwell had been ripped away. But by some miracle, the landing where they stood was still intact. Had they moved any faster, they would probably have been crushed. By stopping to help a woman in need, Jonas and his men made it out alive.

Suggested reading: *The Last Men Out: Life on the Edge at Rescue 2 Firehouse* by Tom Downey
(Henry Holt and Co., 2004)

SEEING EYE DOG STICKS
BY PAL IN WTC HORROR

Blind computer technician Omar Eduardo Rivera was on the seventy-first floor of the World Trade Center's North Tower when terrorists slammed a jet into the building twenty-five floors above him. With smoke, shattered glass, and panicked colleagues all around him, Rivera grabbed the harness of his seeing-eye dog, Salty, and started groping for the exit. The heat and smoke became unbearable, and Rivera doubted that he would make it out. But he wanted to give his service dog, a yellow Labrador retriever, a chance. So he unhooked the harness, and ordered Salty, "Go." The dog was swept away in the crush of people fleeing the doomed skyscraper. Alone, Rivera continued down, his progress much slower without Salty. Suddenly, he felt something nudge his knee. It was Salty, who refused to leave his master behind. The dog guided him down the seventy flights, making it out just before the building collapsed. "It was then I knew for certain he loved me just as much as I loved him," Rivera said. "He was prepared to die in the hope he might save my life."

MESSENGER BATTLES
BLIZZARD AND BULLETS

James Dunigan, who had started working for Western
Union as a messenger boy in the 1850s, risked his life
during the Civil War by carrying government dispatches
and war orders to army posts around New York. In the
winter of 1862, he embarked upon his most hazardous
mission—to deliver a message to a Union commander on
Governor's Island. Because the bay was frozen and a
howling blizzard had roared in, no boats were making the
crossing. So Dunigan and another Western Union boy
began jumping from ice floe to ice floe across the storm-
battered bay. The trip was exhausting, and as the duo
neared their destination, Union soldiers mistook them for
spies and started shooting. Dunigan stayed on course.
When the other courier took a bullet in his hand, the
intrepid messenger carried him until soldiers, realizing
their mistake, pulled the pair from the ice. Dunigan
survived the war and stayed with Western Union until his
death in 1902.

BEACHGOERS RESCUE
RIPTIDE VICTIMS

Screams in the ocean jolted fashion designer Kristin Bledsoe, twenty-three, into action on New York's Rockaway Beach in September 2004. Grabbing a woman's boogie board, she charged into the surf. Two men had been caught in the notoriously perilous Rockaway riptide. Bledsoe, who had spent seven years as a lifeguard, paddled out one hundred yards, followed closely by another Good Samaritan, off-duty firefighter Brian Sullivan. One man had already gone under, but Bledsoe found him by accident when she kicked him while treading water. Sullivan and Bledsoe pulled him up, then held both men above water until emergency personnel arrived on the scene.

HERO FROM HISTORY
George Washington

He would have been perfectly happy as a gentleman farmer at his Mount Vernon, Virginia, plantation, but history had different plans for George Washington, who was born on February 22, 1732. As a young officer fighting for the British in the French and Indian War, he narrowly escaped with his life after twice having his horse shot out from under him. But later, as British rule over its North American colonies grew more onerous, Washington turned against the mother country. In May 1775, he was chosen as commander in chief of the Continental Army, whipping a ragtag bunch of rebels into a formidable fighting force. By 1781, the British surrendered, allowing Washington to turn his eyes back to his farm. But the country needed him more. "Liberty, when it starts to take root, is a plant of rapid growth," he said. In eight years, he sowed the seeds from which America would blossom. He finally retired to his beloved Mount Vernon, but died less than three years later.

COUPLE SHIELDS PHOTOGRAPHER FROM MOB

The streets of Los Angeles erupted into violence in 1992 when a jury declared four cops not guilty in the beating of motorist Rodney King. Photographer Raul Aguilar had the bad luck to pull up in his van to the same intersection where a trucker had nearly been beaten to death earlier that day. Suddenly a rock crashed through Aguilar's window, then a rioter reached into the vehicle. Aguilar tried to run, but the frenzied pack tackled him and beat him. That's when Barbara Henry, who had been watching from her home nearby, took action. Barbara and her husband, James, ran over to the injured Aguilar, warded off the mob, and carried him into their home, where he was safe until police could escort him to a hospital. As the riots wore on, Barbara and James stood in the road, warning motorists of the dangers ahead. "I feel a great sense of responsibility," Barbara said at the time. "We kind of feel like it was our street. Our people. That we were responsible." After two days in a coma, Aguilar recovered. He and the Henrys, who visited him often in the hospital, became good friends.

SWIMMER RESCUES BOATING ACCIDENT VICTIMS IN BIG SURF

Brian V. Frederick, twenty-seven, a graphic artist, couldn't believe his eyes as he gazed from a coastal bluff overlooking Half Moon Bay in California in 2003. In the cold Pacific, Martin Gonzalez, forty-four, and Josue Rodriguez, seven, were thrashing about after their fishing boat had taken on water and sank. Only the little boy had on a lifejacket. Frederick raced down a trail to the beach, stripped off his outer clothes, and, despite the 58-degree water, jumped into the rough surf and swam to Josue, who was being battered by large breakers ninety feet from shore. Grasping Josue by his life jacket, Frederick towed him to shore, then removed the life jacket and donned it himself. He reentered the water and swam about four hundred fifty feet to Gonzalez, who, in high swells beyond the breakers, slipped under the water. But Frederick found him, pulled him to the surface, and kept him afloat until rescuers arrived. Josue and Gonzalez suffered from hypothermia and required hospital treatment. Frederick, who was treated by paramedics for mild hypothermia, suffered cuts and bruised limbs.

DISABLED BOY REACHES MILLIONS THROUGH POETRY

Mattie Stepanek was born with a rare fatal form of muscular dystrophy, but before his death at age thirteen in 2004, he touched and inspired millions. Stepanek started writing poetry at age three as therapy to ease the pain over the death of his brother, who died from the same disease. In 2001, a small publishing house put out a collection of Mattie's poems called *Heartsongs*. It quickly zoomed to the top of the *New York Times* bestseller list. Mattie was confined to a wheelchair and needed a ventilator, feeding tube, blood transfusions, and repeated hospitalizations. Through it all, he kept writing and remained upbeat and happy. Four more books won him fans around the world, including Oprah Winfrey, who found inspiration in his verses. "Mattie was something special, something very special," said Jerry Lewis, chairman of the Muscular Dystrophy Foundation. "His example made people want to reach for the best in themselves."

For more information: www.myhero.com

TEAMWORK FREES ELDERLY DRIVER FROM FLAMING PICKUP

In an accident in 2003, Clifford Gandy's pickup truck hurtled across a lawn in Elk Grove, California, and slammed into a home, severing a gas line. The escaping gas ignited, and flames spread to Gandy's truck, which was embedded in the wall of the house. Neighbors Lawrence Gonzi, fifty-three, and Olga Renee Rosander, forty-eight, sprang into action. Rosander didn't even take the time to put on her shoes and ran through the wreck barefoot. Gonzi pushed past the flames and reached into the cab where Gandy, seventy, was unconscious. Gonzi had to cut the safety belt before he could yank Gandy free, and, with Rosander's help, dragged the elderly man across the street as fire destroyed the truck and much of the house.

SMALL BOY PULLS
SINKING GRANDDAD
FROM MUCK

"Give me the strength!" shouted ten-year-old Billy Birch after his grandfather slipped and tumbled into a canal in Witton, England, in 2004. "I went into the water and it was up to my waist," Billy's grandfather, also named Billy, told reporters. "I was sinking deeper in the mud and slime and couldn't get out, so I called Billy." The boy weighed only sixty-three pounds, but he summoned the strength to yank his 182-pound grandfather out of the mud and to safety. "I'm so proud of him," said Billy's mother, Dawn. "He just seems to be a natural hero." In fact, this was Billy's second experience at lifesaving. Back in 2002, he rescued his baby sister after she fell in a pool.

MOM AND TOT OWE LIVES TO QUICK-THINKING RESCUERS

Lindsay M. Ryder, twenty-two, and her son, Evan Moody, three, were trapped after her car hurtled down an embankment and crashed into a tree near Canaan, Maine, in September 2003. Mark Potter, forty-two, a dental equipment technician, and David Lee Custer, forty-five, a courier, heard the accident and ran to the scene. They yanked open the driver's door and pulled Ryder out then rushed back to get Evan, who was in a safety seat. Custer held the door open, while Potter cut the straps holding the safety seat and freed the baby. They scrambled up the embankment seconds before the car burst into flames.

DOG FINDS BOY BURIED UNDER COLLAPSED WALL

One afternoon in 1940, Tim, an eight-year-old German shepherd, was strolling along a street in New York with his master, John Nuccio. Meanwhile, a potential tragedy was unfolding a block away. The rear wall of a tenement collapsed, burying Charles Bossman, eleven. The boy lay under the bricks and rubble, with no one aware that he was trapped and nearly suffocating. But Tim smelled trouble. The dog ran to the scene and started digging furiously in the debris until Nuccio and others found the boy and pulled him alive from the rubble. Later that year Tim was given an award for his actions. The medal read: "To Tim, a Dog, for Saving the Life of a Boy."

FARMHAND TAKES BULL BY HORNS IN RESCUE

Warren A. Deacon, a forty-seven-year-old farmer in Ascot, Quebec, was leading a twenty-six-hundred-pound bull in a pasture in 1994. Suddenly, without warning, the bull whirled around and butted Deacon to the ground, then started stomping him. Deacon screamed to hired hand Michael Naylor for help. Naylor, twenty-three, had been repairing a nearby fence, so he grabbed the hammer he was using and ran to where Deacon lay helpless. Naylor whacked the bull in the head until it got mad and started chasing him. Naylor dashed off with the bull in hot pursuit. But a few seconds later, it turned around and continued its attack on Deacon. Back came Naylor with the hammer, slamming away at the raging bull. This time he diverted the animal's attention long enough to allow Deacon to scramble into a cattle feeder. Once again, the bull left Naylor and went after Deacon, slamming the feeder. Meanwhile, Naylor hopped into Deacon's truck and drove straight at the bull before it stopped its attack and ran off. Deacon scrambled into the truck and Naylor sped to the hospital. Naylor's bullfighting bravery earned him a Carnegie Hero award.

For more information: carnegiehero.org

JOCKEY HERO OF SMALL PLANE CRASH

Something went terribly wrong as a twin-propeller Piper Seneca carrying jockeys Frankie Dettori and Ray Cochrane was taking off from an airstrip next to the Newmarket Racecourse in Sussex, England, in 2000. The plane started shaking violently and then nose-dived into the ground. The jockeys and pilot Patrick Mackey were trapped in the burning wreckage. With the main door jammed, Cochrane crawled through a baggage door, yelling at Dettori to follow him. Once outside, Cochrane helped Dettori, who had broken his ankle, to a safe distance from the wreckage, which was now on fire. "While I was clearing my vision I could see Ray going back to the plane," recalled Dettori. "He had taken his jacket off and was trying to fight the flames." But Cochrane couldn't save the pilot. A few months later, the Royal Humane Society presented the Irish jockey with an award for bravery. "It's very nice, but really I'm not a hero," Cochrane said. "People were in trouble and needed help, and I was the only one there to do something."

"The ordinary man is involved in action, the hero acts. An immense difference."

—Henry Miller, author

PASSERBY RUNS INTO FLAMING HOUSE TO SAVE WOMAN

When fire broke out in her kitchen in 2002, Brenda Gregory, thirty-eight, became disoriented and was trapped in the bathroom as thick smoke filled her house in Welland, Ontario. Suddenly she heard a man's voice. "Pound on the floor!" he yelled. She pounded as hard as she could and in seconds the man, Dennis J. Rogers, a thirty-seven-year-old machinist, grabbed her wrists and dragged her into the cold night air and safety. Rogers had been passing by in a car and, noticing flames, dashed into the burning house to rescue a stranger.

HOLLYWOOD HEROES
STAR IN CRASH RESCUE

When Colin Specht was trapped inside a flaming Jeep Cherokee in Brentwood, California in 1996, it was like a scene out of the movies, complete with Hollywood heroes. Specht, sixteen, was a passenger in the vehicle driven by his friend Erik McMurrow, also sixteen, when it flipped over and caught fire. McMurrow pulled himself out of the window, but Specht was caught inside. Actor Mark Harmon, star of the TV drama *St. Elsewhere*, and his wife, actress Pam Dawber, ran from their home across the street and leapt into action. Together they braved the flames and smashed the passenger-side window with a sledgehammer, pulled the teenager from the car, and rolled him on the grass to smother the flames that were searing his lower body. "I just acted instinctively," said Harmon.

PIT BULL FINDS
ABANDONED INFANT
ON ROOF

Tonya Williams of Brooklyn was never too fond of Princess, the big canine companion of her twelve-year-old daughter, Yashima. That all changed in October 2004 when the pit bull–boxer mix made an unusual discovery. That morning when Yashima opened the door to take Princess for a walk, the dog bolted out of the Williams's apartment and scampered up to the sixth-floor landing. There on the floor was a newborn baby boy, his umbilical cord still attached. Princess started licking the baby's face, warming him. Yashima called her mother, who wrapped the baby up and called 911. "I always wanted to get rid of that dog," Williams said. "Now, I'll keep her forever." The baby survived and was put in state custody.

WINDSURFER RESCUES FIVE TRAPPED IN SINKING PLANE

A Sunday evening dinner turned into a dramatic rescue by a Long Island graphic designer in July 2003. Peter Johnson, thirty-eight, was in the middle of a leisurely meal with his cousin, Gale Leddy, when they saw a small plane plunge into the Great Peconic Bay. While his cousin called police, Johnson grabbed a windsurfing board and paddled out to the wreck. The four passengers and pilot were alive, but trapped in the sinking plane. Johnson helped them break out and guided them back to land. Then, without a word, he vanished. Newspapers dubbed him the mystery hero, but when he surfaced a few days later, he said he had to hurry away to meet his wife. His cousin, however, said that he was just a modest guy and didn't want any attention. "He thinks he just did what anyone would do," she said. All the occupants of the plane escaped with minor injuries.

DEPUTIES DASH THROUGH INFERNO FOR STRANDED GRANNY

Two sheriff's deputies sped through a scene out of hell as a forest fire threatened to kill an elderly woman who lived in a cabin in a canyon near Upton, California, in 2002. John Rose II, thirty-two, and Paul Archambault, forty-three, drove around smoldering trees, over scorched earth, and in smoke so dense they could barely make out the road to reach Sigrid Szymczak-Hopson, seventy, whose cabin was directly in the path of the raging inferno. At one point, the road narrowed to one lane with a three-hundred-foot drop on the side. When they reached the cabin, Rose sprinted to the door while Archambault stayed behind the wheel and kept the engine running for a speedy getaway. Two of their tires blew out during their wild ride back through the fire, but all three made it to safety, with no injuries.

Suggested reading: *A Season of Fire: Four Months on the Firelines in the American West* by Doug Gantenbein (J. P. Tarcher/Penguin, 2003)

"Without heroes we're all plain people and don't know how far we can go."

—Bernard Malamud, American novelist

HARE RAISES ALARM
ON PROWLER

Francesca, a fluffy eight-pound rabbit, played the role
of guard dog in a real-life crime drama in 1987 in
Bloomington, Indiana. As her owner, college student
Kate Stanley, slumbered soundly, Francesca climbed up on
a bedside stool, jumped on Kate, and started pounding
with her powerful hind legs and yanking at the covers
with her teeth. Kate woke up and heard noises outside
her bedroom window. The sleepy girl walked into the
kitchen to investigate and was about to open the back
door when Francesca bit her on the ankle. "That brought
me to my senses," she said. After that there was silence
outside, so Kate went back to bed. Francesca huddled
close to her all night. The next day, Kate reported the
incident to the police, who found marks on her window,
suggesting that someone had tried to break in. They also
told her that a knife-wielding intruder had attacked a
neighbor at about the same time that Kate's hare raised
the alarm.

SUPERMAN INSPIRES WORLD AFTER PARALYZING ACCIDENT

Christopher Reeve played Superman on the silver screen, but after a devastating horseback-riding accident in 1995, the movie star showed the world the heart of a real hero. The strapping six-foot-four actor was paralyzed from the neck down. Reeve first thought of suicide, but decided instead to fight against a villain more sinister than any screenwriters could cook up. Reeve astounded doctors by pushing his own body so hard he achieved things that the best medical minds deemed impossible, such as moving his finger. He became a tireless campaigner for research into spinal cord injury, raising millions of dollars and worldwide awareness for the problem. Never giving in, Reeve was resolved to walk again and his optimism inspired other paralyzed patients to try just a little harder. Through lobbying, his foundation, and two autobiographies—*Still Me* and *Nothing Is Impossible*—he spread his message of hope around the world. Sadly, Reeve died in 2004 at age fifty-two. But the research started by his campaign may one day help other paralysis victims leave their wheelchairs behind.

For more information: www.christopherreeve.org

PARALYZED BULL TERRIER PROTECTS PUPS IN FIRE

Old and half paralyzed, Topsy the bull terrier was a lifesaver when fire broke out in a New York boarding house for dogs in 1905. Even though she could only crawl, Topsy was determined to save her two puppies. By the time she managed to pick up the first one, the only exit was blocked by fire. So she dragged herself and her pups, one by one, into a room that the blaze had not yet reached. As the fire threatened her sanctuary, Topsy climbed up on a sofa and tried to dig a hole in the cushion to hide her pups. Just then, firefighters entered the flaming room and crowded around the sofa where Topsy was frantically digging to make the hole big enough for the three of them. Firemen carried Topsy and her pups to safety and pampered them until the next morning, when the dogs were reunited with their owner.

DRIVER IN SUBCOMPACT STOPS RUNAWAY SUV

Jerod Shane Wilson, thirty, didn't waste any time after seeing that the driver of the SUV in front of him had passed out, causing the vehicle to speed out of control on an interstate highway near Hayden, Alabama, in 1999. As the SUV entered the median and repeatedly struck a concrete barrier, Wilson pulled his subcompact car in front of the runaway and slowed down, allowing the vehicle, which weighed twice as much as his, to strike the rear of his car. After the SUV repeatedly hit Wilson's car, both veered across the highway and struck a guide rail. Just then another driver positioned his loaded delivery truck in front of both vehicles and brought them to a stop. The driver of the SUV, Kara Roberts, twenty-eight, escaped injury. Wilson, whose vehicle was badly damaged, was hospitalized for neck, hip, and back injuries but made a full recovery. For his bravery, he earned a Carnegie Hero award.

For more information: carnegiehero.org

HERO FROM HISTORY
Ida Lewis

As the first woman lighthouse keeper in America, Ida Lewis spent her lifetime rescuing others. She started as a teenager, helping her father with his duties at the Lime Rock lighthouse in Newport, Rhode Island. When he fell ill, Ida, then fifteen, willingly took up the oars. She made her first rescue that year—four young men whose boat had capsized. Her fame spread as she made one rescue after another, each more daring than the last. "In danger, look for the dark-haired girl in the rowboat and follow her," seamen told each other. In 1881, she was awarded the Coast Guard's Gold Lifesaving Medal for rescuing two soldiers who had slipped through broken ice near the lighthouse. Hearing their cries for help, Ida grabbed a rope, ran over the brittle ice, and single-handedly pulled the first man from the water. Her brother aided her in the rescue of the other soldier. Ida stayed for fifty-five years and was credited with saving at least twenty-five people, the last in 1904 when she was a spry sixty-five.

"I'm sure heroes don't go around thinking, 'Hope I can find a good excuse to get out of this.'"

—John Marsden, Australian author

SAILOR RISKS LIFE
TRYING TO SAVE TWO
IN SUBMERGED BOAT

In the fall of 2000, retired firefighter Ronald May was cruising away from Catalina Island in his pleasure boat, the *Mystic,* when he spotted a sinking twenty-three-foot vessel, the *Charades*, about a mile ahead. He arrived just in time to see the stern go under, dumping four of the six terrified boaters into the water. After they grabbed ropes that May had tossed out, he realized that two more passengers—eight-year-old Donta Perry and his sixty-six-year-old grandmother, Mildred Griffin—were trapped inside the submerged cabin. May got his snorkel and fins and plunged into the water to the cabin where he found Griffin and her grandson pinned under some cabinets. May tried three times to free them but was soon forced back to the surface. He returned to his boat and set off a flare, alerting Harbor Patrol. Neither Griffin nor Perry survived. Although May was awarded the Coast Guard's Gold Lifesaving Medal, his thoughts were with the two who died. "I did my best," he said. "But it still bothers me that I couldn't save them."

STUDENT RESCUES TWO
FROM BLAZE

Medical student Thomas Bui was walking home after a grueling twenty-four-hour shift at Queens Hospital Center in New York in 2004 when he heard screams coming from a house three doors from his home in Briarwood. "Fire!" a woman shouted from the balcony of the burning building. Bui ran into the house and rushed out seconds later with a baby. Then he dashed in again, emerging this time with a child before running in a third time. He reached the screaming woman, Maribel Hernandez, as the fire flared inside, forcing the pair to jump from the second-floor balcony. "I don't remember thinking anything at the time," Bui recalled. "I just reacted." People who knew the doctor-in-training were not surprised by his heroism. "He's an amazing person," said his supervisor at the hospital.

CANINE SOLDIER
TACKLES MOB IN BOSNIA

In 2002, Sam, a canine soldier with Britain's Royal Army Veterinary Corps Dog Unit, earned the Dickin Medal, an award given for valor among military animal heroes. While patrolling in Dvar, Bosnia and Herzegovina, in 1998, Sam chased a gunman who had opened fire on innocent people in the town that had been wracked by violent clashes between the Croats and Serbs. The big German shepherd leapt on the gunman and brought him to the ground, allowing his handler, Corporal Iain Carnegie, to disarm the man. Less than a week later as full-scale riots raged throughout Dvar, Carnegie and Sam guarded a compound where a group of ethnic Serbs had taken refuge. An angry mob threatened the Serbs with bottles, rocks, and crowbars, but Sam kept them at bay. "Sam displayed outstanding courage and not once did he shy away from danger," recalled Carnegie. "I could never have carried out my duties without Sam at my side."

For more information: www.pdsa.org.uk

VOLUNTEER DRAGS ZOOKEEPER FROM JAWS OF DEATH

Hannah Lynn Goorsky, twenty-three, had just started volunteering at a zoo in Sacramento, California, in 2003 and had no idea that her duties would include pulling a man from the jaws of death. On her third day on the job, Hannah saw zookeeper Chad Summers, thirty, about to close the tiger cage when the 320-pound beast inside leapt on him, knocked him to the ground, and began mauling him. Goorsky grabbed a shovel and started whacking the tiger over the head, allowing Summers to scramble out of the den to safety.

MAN SNATCHES COWORKER FROM KNIFEMAN

Liam Clatworthy, twenty-four, and Ellen Pemberton, nineteen, were working at a fish-and-chips shop in Bridgend, England, when a man started to walk behind the counter. "Sorry, you can't come behind here," Clatworthy said. The man then grabbed Pemberton, pulled a knife, and held a four-inch blade to her throat. "Give me the money," he snarled, "or I'll stab you." In a flash, Clatworthy leapt at the knifeman and pulled Pemberton away. Together they bolted from the shop as Clatworthy yanked his cell phone from his pocket to call police, who soon caught the armed robber. "If Liam hadn't pulled me away from the man when he did I don't know what would have happened," said Pemberton. "So I would say he's a hero."

"Real heroes are men who fall
and fail and are flawed,
but win out in the end because
they've stayed true to their ideals and
beliefs and commitments."

—Kevin Costner, actor

TEACHER IN PJS SAVES NEIGHBOR FROM EXPLODING HOUSE

Walls blew out and the ceiling collapsed when gas exploded in the living room of the second floor apartment of Isaac W. Bradburn, seventy, late one October night in 2002. A teacher living nearby, Craig Allen Cross, thirty-two, felt the explosion and heard Bradburn's desperate cries for help. Barefoot and in pajamas, Cross sprinted to the scene, entering the house through the gap where the walls used to be, and crawled over mounds of hot debris to the second floor. There he found Bradburn, burned and dazed. Carrying the old man through the fire, Cross got Bradburn out of the building seconds before it was completely engulfed in flames.

For more information: www.carnegiehero.org

VOLUNTEER GRANDMA SPEEDS INFANT RECOVERY

Rayshon Modeste was a sick infant, born in 2003 with serious breathing problems. In the first six months of his life, he had to stay in Kings County Hospital in Brooklyn where doctors tended to his physical problems. But Rayshon needed more. That's when Khadijah Ali came to the rescue. Ali is part of the Foster Grandparents Program, which brings seniors and needy children together. Ali was assigned to comfort Rayshon with songs, hugs, and human touch, as he was subjected to procedures and examinations in the cold sterile hospital environment. Over the years, the elderly woman has been a volunteer grandma for sixty babies in the hospital's neonatal unit. "I've never had a child, so being with these babies, sitting with them, nurturing them, and bonding with them—it means so much to me," she said.

For more information: http://www.seniorcorps.gov/

DOG PHONES 911,
OPENS DOOR FOR COPS

Faith, a four-year-old Rottweiler, was a service dog for Leana Beasley, forty-five, who suffers from grand mal seizures. The dog had been trained to sense changes in Beasley's blood chemistry and warn of an impending attack. But something went terribly wrong in 2004 when Beasley passed out and fell out of her wheelchair. Faith sprang into action. She knocked the phone off the hook then, as she'd been taught to do, hit the speed dial for 911. When the operator answered, the dog barked with such urgency that the operator had to act. "The dog was too persistent in barking directly into the phone receiver. I knew she was trying to tell me something," said dispatcher Jenny Buchanan. She traced the call and sent help. When the police arrived, the smart dog unlocked the front door for the officer. Beasley's doctors determined that the woman had a bad reaction to her seizure medications and might have died if she didn't have Faith.

DAD AND GOOD SAMARITAN CRAWL THROUGH FLAMES FOR TOTS

Five members of the Vargas family ran outside when fire raced through their home in Lompoc, California, in 2002, before they realized that one-year-old Jullian and three-year-old Marissa were still inside. Jose Flores, twenty-one, a cabinetmaker who was visiting a friend in a neighboring house, saw the blaze and sprang into action. Along with the children's father, Flores entered the smoke-filled house and crawled into the living room, snatched Marissa, and led her outside. Meanwhile, the children's father found Jullian and carried him safely out of the burning house.

PAL PLUCKS ANGLER
FROM RAGING RIVER

Teenagers Ben Wyatt and Percy Vleitman were heading out on a river near Walpole, Massachusetts, in 2004 for a day of fishing when a swell broke the steering cable of their small motorboat. Then rough waters caused Vleitman, who was wearing fishing waders, to fall overboard into the swirling current. By maneuvering the outboard motor by hand, Wyatt was able to steer the boat and headed after his friend who was thrashing in the rushing river. Wyatt finally got close enough to throw a lifejacket and rope to Vleitman, but it was too risky to bring him aboard. So Wyatt jumped into the water, swam to his floundering buddy, and guided him to a rock where they waited until help arrived. Claiming that Wyatt saved his life, Vleitman said he had become exhausted trying to free himself from his heavy fishing waders and had just about used up his last bit of strength when Wyatt rescued him.

"Success is achievable without public recognition, and the world has many unsung heroes."

—Michael DeBakey, MD, heart surgeon

MECHANIC DIVES THROUGH FLAMES TO FREE TRAPPED MAN

A gas explosion blew the roof off of Alex McKay's house in Lake Wales, Florida, in 2002. McKay, eighty-four, was trapped on the side porch by flaming debris, and his clothes were on fire. Jimmie Michael Acerman, fifty-three, a mechanic who was working nearby, rushed to the house and scaled the flaming rubble to reach McKay. After using his cap to snuff out McKay's burning clothes, Acerman hoisted the elderly man to rescuers and then jumped out of the house himself as fire consumed the building. Sadly, despite Acerman's heroic actions, McKay died from burns the next day.

PARTY DOG PLAYS REAL-LIFE ANGEL

After she slipped into an icy river near Richland, Washington, in 2002, Dragica Vlaco lay on the riverbank, thinking she had died because she saw a halo and wings. But this was no ordinary angel. It had four legs, a cold nose, and a long tail. His name was Buoy—a yellow Labrador retriever decked out in a costume for a Halloween party. Buoy's owner, Jim Simpson, had let the pooch outside earlier that evening. When the usually obedient dog didn't return, Simpson went looking for him. He found Buoy on the riverbank huddled next to Vlaco, who was soaking wet and shivering in 20-degree weather. Vlaco had become disoriented after taking a pain medication and wandered off. Her distraught family had been searching for her for hours. Authorities said that in the freezing cold, Vlaco might not have survived much longer if it hadn't been for Buoy. She recovered after being treated for hypothermia.

PASSERBY SAVES MOTORIST FROM BEING CRUSHED

Driving his car in downtown Montreal in 1996, Gerard Gravel, fifty, stopped in traffic beneath an overpass. Suddenly, Gravel found himself being crushed by falling chunks of concrete. Above him, a loaded dump truck had gone out of control on the overpass and broken through the side wall, sending large pieces of rock and concrete onto Gravel's car. The falling rubble demolished the car and jammed and blocked its doors, trapping Gravel inside. Meanwhile, the truck itself remained suspended above him, dangling over the side of the overpass. As it continued dropping more of its cargo onto Gravel's car, he shouted for help. Just then Marie-Eve Renaud, a twenty-two-year-old college student, arrived. She could see that the teetering truck could fall at any moment, but she ran up to Gravel's car anyway. Despite being pelted with falling debris, she shoved chunks out of the way and, with all her might, yanked open the driver's door and helped Gravel crawl out. They fled to safety.

THIRD ATTEMPT IS
CHARM FOR RESCUER

The old saying, "If at first you don't succeed, try, try again," has special meaning for a rescuer and the woman he saved. Denise Robinson, a thirty-nine-year-old disabled woman, was trapped in her burning house in Summit, New York, in 2003. Off-duty emergency medical technician William J. Lum, twenty-four, ran to the house after he saw smoke. Noxious fumes nearly knocked him out on his first attempt to get inside. The second time, visibility was so poor that he slammed into a support beam and staggered out of the house. The third time, he crouched and made it into the living room where Robinson was on the floor. Lum grabbed her ankle and pulled her outside, using his body to shield her from falling debris and heat-shattered glass. After treatment for smoke inhalation, both recovered.

ENRAGED CITIZEN
CHASES BANK ROBBERS

First the two robbers used a car as a battering ram to get into an ATM machine at a bank in London just before it opened in 2003. Then they scurried off, carrying a cash box. Witnessing the heist, Cameron Black, sixty-four, chased them on foot. "I was totally aware of what I was doing, just angry to see people breaking the law," recalled Black. While he ran after them, the robber carrying the cash box tripped and fell. Black tried to kick the cash box under a parked car. At that moment the other crook pulled a gun and fired at Black, who was so mad that he didn't even realize he had been shot until he saw blood on his shirt. Fortunately, the wound was minor. Despite Black's heroic chase, the bad guys got away with the money.

"True heroism is remarkably sober, very undramatic. It is not the urge to surpass all others at whatever cost, but the urge to serve others at whatever cost."

—Arthur Ashe, tennis star

CHARITY BEGINS AT THIRTY THOUSAND FEET FOR FLIGHT ATTENDANT

Nancy Rivard was rising through management at American Airlines when her father died of cancer in 1983. Heartbroken, Rivard asked for a demotion to flight attendant, which would give her a low-cost way to search the world for some meaning in her life. She soon came up with the idea of getting volunteers the same travel privileges as airline employees so they could deliver aid to the needy all over the world. She convinced other flight attendants to make small gestures, like collecting hotel soaps and shampoos and delivering them to Bosnian refugees. Eventually, four thousand volunteers in and out of the airline industry took up Rivard's cause, using flight passes to personally deliver ten million dollars' worth of goods to the needy. Today, members escort orphans to new adoptive families and hand-deliver humanitarian aid to orphanages, clinics, and remote communities. "When you do good work, the doors keep opening," Rivard said.

For more information: www.airlineamb.org

SIZE DOESN'T MATTER TO YOUNG CRIME FIGHTERS

When George Ball and John McMahon heard the screams of a damsel in distress on a London street in 2004, they didn't hesitate to come to her aid. It didn't matter that at just nine years old, they were each about half the size of the six-foot man who had mugged a young woman and stolen her expensive Cartier watch. The pint-sized crime busters charged after the thief and grabbed him around the ankles. Figuring he was outmatched, the thief dropped his loot and scrammed. The boy wonders, who were later honored with a Champion Children award, calmly picked up the watch and returned it to the damsel, who was dumbfounded but no longer in distress.

DOG FISHES FRIENDS
FROM ICY LAKE

Dog trainer Jim Gilchrist, sixty-one, of Innisfil, Ontario, was walking across a frozen lake in 1995 when the ice cracked open and he plunged into the frigid water. His dogs—Tara, a Rottweiler, and Tiree, a golden retriever—charged to the rescue. Tara reached him first but fell in also. Seeing both her companions in trouble, Tiree took a different approach. She went down on her belly and crept up to the hole in the ice, allowing Gilchrist to grab her collar. But Tiree would not have been able to haul her two-hundred-pound master out of the water alone. Sensing this, Tara scrambled up on Gilchrist's back and jumped out of the water. Then she got down on her belly and sidled up to the hole right next to Tiree. Gilchrist grabbed their collars and the dogs backed up, pulling him to safety. "The dogs risked their lives to save me," Gilchrist said later. All three recovered, but Tara remained forever fearful of water.

ATTORNEY LAYS DOWN LAW TO BACK-ALLEY BRUTE

Attorney Ronald Gross, thirty-one, heard screams as he was driving along a city street in York, Pennsylvania, in 2003 and saw a man dragging a struggling woman, Kelly A. Capitani, thirty-four, into an alley. Gross jumped out of his car and yelled at the brute to leave the woman alone. The assailant turned, giving Capitani the chance to break free. She dove into Gross's car while her attacker whipped out a pellet gun, pointed it at Gross, and forced him down to the pavement. He threatened to kill Gross, but whacked him in the jaw instead and sauntered off. Gross wasted no time in calling cops, who tracked the assailant down and killed him in a gun battle.

CHAMPION SWIMMER'S DARING DIVE KEEPS SHIP AFLOAT

O f the Winged Footers, the swift athletes of the New York Athletic Club, none was faster in the water than swimmer Tedford Cann. When he traded the sporting arena for the battlefield in World War I, his swimming prowess made him a hero. Cann was a sailor aboard the *U.S.S. May* in 1917, when the ship was involved in an accident and started to sink in the North Atlantic. The champion volunteered to dive to the bottom of the bilge and plug up the dangerous leak. No one knew the size of the hole or if Cann would be sucked under. With the water rising in the hull from seven to eight feet, Cann dove into the black water. He quickly found the hole and returned to the hatch for some cork to plug it up. It took several trips and more than an hour, but soon the leak was closed. Cann's daring dive saved the ship and earned the young athlete the Medal of Honor.

For more information on Medals of Honor:
www.cmohs.org

GIRL LEADS HORSES FROM BURNING STABLE

While Ashley Martinez, sixteen, was alone, cleaning stalls in a Staten Island, New York, stable in 2003, a huge blast literally raised the roof and blew in the windows. A barge offloading gasoline at an Exxon Mobil facility nearby had exploded and the smoke and sparks were filling the stable, causing it to catch fire. Ashley, a champion equestrienne, was scared, but she knew she had to get the animals out of the stable. She also knew that it would not be easy to move sixteen fear-crazed horses on her own. But the stable owner was not home so Ashley had no choice. One by one, starting with her favorite, a twenty-four-year-old pony named Pearl, Ashley led all of the horses out of the burning stable to safety.

FRIEND FOILS KNIFE-WIELDING ATTACKER

One evening in 2002, Cheryl-Ann Moriarty, twenty-eight, a machinist from Nashua, New Hampshire, received a frantic phone call from a friend. Rebecca McKenzie was having a violent argument in her apartment with a man she knew and asked Moriarty to come and pick her up. By the time Moriarty arrived, the argument had turned into a knife attack behind a locked door. In desperation, Moriarty broke through two doors to get in and found McKenzie bleeding on the living room floor, her attacker hovering over her with a knife. Moriarty grabbed his shoulder to yank him away, but he stabbed her in the left arm. "I'll kill you!" he bellowed as she fled into the kitchen. He stabbed her three more times, twice in the arm, once in the back, before she wrenched the weapon from his hand and fled the apartment to call police, who nabbed the attacker. Both women recovered, although McKenzie was in the hospital for two weeks.

CAT SOUNDS FIRE ALARM

Charlie was a big, old, fat Burmese cat, but that didn't stop him from becoming a hero. Although the ten-year-old feline lived outdoors most of the time, owners Ken and Kimberly Coleman of Pensacola, Florida, brought him into the house because of cold weather in November 1991. Just before midnight, Charlie jumped on Kimberly, clawing her face. She woke to smell smoke from a fire that had broken out in the chimney. The couple, their twin babies, and Charlie all made it out to safety. Fire officials say the blaze could have been a killer had Charlie not been on the alert.

NEIGHBOR SAVES MAN
FROM ELECTROCUTION

While going for a walk on a snowy day in 1958 in Baltimore, Eduard Althausen, sixty-three, watched neighbor Gerhard Erlemann, sixty, shovel snow in an alley in front of his garage. Just then Erlemann uncovered a fallen power line which had snapped off a nearby utility pole during a heavy snowfall the day before. Not realizing what it was, he picked up the live wire, which carried twenty-four hundred volts of electricity, and immediately lost consciousness, falling backward to the ground. Althausen, who had a cardiac condition, rushed to his side. With his hands protected only by fur-lined leather gloves, Althausen grabbed the wire and, despite feeling a strong tingle, jerked twice on the wire, freeing it from Erlemann's grasp. The victim, who was rushed to the hospital where he regained consciousness six hours later, suffered a fractured shoulder blade and a severe burn on the palm of his hand. He was hospitalized for a month. Althausen's heart suffered no ill effects from his heroism.

SOLDIER BEATS BACK
JAPANESE IN BURMA

The fighting had been fierce in the Burmese jungle in 1944 as the Japanese tried to cross from Burma into India before the start of the monsoon season. Agansing Rai was an acting corporal in the Fifth Royal Gurkha Rifles—soldiers from Nepal fighting for the British in Burma. His company had been ordered to recapture two outposts that had been taken by the Japanese. As the Gurkhas approached the first outpost, they were pinned down by heavy machine-gun fire. Watching his comrades fall, Rai realized he had to destroy the machine-gun nest. With his men, Rai dashed across eighty yards and killed the four soldiers manning the gun. Then Rai and his squad charged and destroyed another nest, but Rai lost almost half of his men. Armed with a grenade and a sub-machine gun, Rai single-handedly killed four Japanese soldiers who were firing from a bunker. For his bravery and initiative, Rai won the Victoria Cross, the British Army's highest medal for valor.

"Courage is not simply one of the virtues, but the form of every virtue at the testing point."

—C. S. Lewis, author

SOCIAL WORKER SAVES THIRTY-FIVE HUNDRED DOGS AND CATS

Three decades ago Chitra Besbroda was a social worker in Harlem when she noticed that the slums were just as hard on animals as they were on people. "Some of them [were] in the most gruesome conditions," she said. "I even found a skeleton of a dog still tied with his collar and leash on—a total skeleton with just bare bones left. The dog had died of starvation." She decided to devote her life to helping the neighborhood's junkyard dogs, establishing the nonprofit organization Sentient Creatures in 1994. In her nearly thirty years working with homeless and abused animals, she has found homes for more than thirty-five hundred dogs and cats. Many of these animals would have died without the care and training Chitra gave them.

For more information: www.sentientcreatures.org

LIFESAVER LEANS ON GARDEN HOSE

Three-year-old Ricardo Monteiro was somewhere in his family's burning house in Sacramento, California, in 2002, but his rescuers couldn't find him. Learning of the emergency, Gabriel Gherle, a twenty-five-year-old construction worker, broke a window to get in, but he had to retreat when he failed to find Ricardo in the front of the house. Gherle ran around to the back, where he found a garden hose and doused himself with water. Then, lugging the hose with him, he dashed back into the smoke and fire. He found Ricardo unconscious on the floor, sprayed water on him, picked him up, and then quickly got out of the blaze. Gherle handed Ricardo to rescue workers who rushed the boy to the hospital, where he made a full recovery.

GREAT DANE CHASES GUNMEN FROM BAR

When eight armed robbers entered John Goetz's cabaret in Summit, Illinois, the day before Thanksgiving in 1930, they didn't notice the crime buster dozing behind the bar. Kaiser, Goetz's pet Great Dane, stayed hidden while the gunmen forced the patrons to line up against a wall with their hands in the air. Suddenly a police officer who had been in the restroom came out with his gun blazing. One of the robbers turned off the lights while the other crooks started firing wildly. That's when Kaiser attacked. He grabbed one of the men and held on until a bullet ripped into his shoulder. But Kaiser refused to quit. He followed the flashes from the guns and repeatedly attacked the robbers, sinking his teeth into their legs. He was still hanging onto a gunman's coattail when his adversaries fled through the door. Three people died and three were wounded in the attack, but the toll might have been much worse without Kaiser. The dog was only slightly wounded by the shot and rewarded for his courage with a big helping of Thanksgiving turkey.

HERO FROM HISTORY
Andrei Sakharov

Andrei Sakharov was a decorated Soviet physicist developing atomic weapons during the Cold War. He eventually realized that the ideals he had pursued as a scientist—compassion, freedom, and truth—could not thrive in an arms race or under communism. He campaigned for disarmament and denounced the Soviet system and its intolerance of dissent. When his words of opposition spread throughout the world, he was put under house arrest and became estranged from his children. For his courage, he received the Nobel Peace Prize in 1975, but in 1980, he was exiled to the remote city of Gorky. Still, he refused to be silenced and was finally released in 1986. By courageously speaking the truth, Sakharov became the conscience of the Cold War and inspired the movement that toppled Soviet communism.

For more information:
www.nobelprize.org/peace/laureates/1975/
sakharov-autobio.html

U.S. AIRMAN RESCUES 27 IN DEVASTATING FLOODS

R aging waters whipped through the English coastal town of Hunstanton in the devastating floods of 1953, said to be the worst peacetime disaster to hit Great Britain in the twentieth century. When the waters roared up from the North Sea, American airman Reis Leming, stationed at the U.S. Air base in Sculthorpe, grabbed a small rubber raft and plunged all alone through the darkness and the huge waves. Hearing screams and cries for help from the trapped and dying, Leming quickly went to work aiding stranded people off roofs and taking them to higher ground. "It was cold, bitterly cold," he recalled. "And there came a time when I realized that I, too, was probably not going to survive." He rescued twenty-seven people before collapsing from hypothermia. When he came to hours later, the first words he heard were, "Cut off his legs." Fortunately, the voice was that of a nurse trying to get the legs off his flight suit so she could massage him back to life. Leming became the first American in peacetime to win Britain's George Medal for gallantry, the nation's second-highest honor.

YOUNGSTER TAKES
CHARGE IN FAMILY FIRE

On a November morning in 2003, ten-year-old Dean Kerr of West Edinburgh, Scotland, saw smoke and flames coming from the room of his sister Leigh, nine. Making sure she was out, he slammed the door and phoned up the fire brigade. "The woman asked if I could get my family out of the house so I said I would try," he recalled. He woke his parents, then went to get his brother. "My little brother wouldn't get out of his bed so I picked him up," Dean said later. "He was crying and I took him downstairs and we all got out okay." The local fire commander said that had Dean not acted so quickly it's likely that someone in the house might have been seriously injured or died.

HEART TRANSPLANT
PATIENT
DISARMS GUNMAN

Lyle D. Baade, sixty-six, a retired construction worker living in a Peoria, Arizona, retirement community, was a heart transplant recipient, but he still had the strength to prevent a massacre in 2000. Richard Glassel, sixty-six, had barged into the center's meeting room where forty members of the homeowner's association had assembled. He had three loaded pistols and a loaded assault rifle. Glassel, a disgruntled former resident of the community, raised one of the pistols and started firing, striking four. When he put the pistol down and started picking up the assault rifle, Baade sprinted across the foyer. Even though Glassel outweighed him significantly, Baade managed to wrestle the gunman to the ground, where they struggled for control of the weapon. Glassel got off one wild shot, which hit another man in the ankle. But then other men in the room followed Baade's lead and jumped on Glassel and restrained him until cops arrived. Two women died in the attack and three were wounded, but Baade, who had to be treated for a rapid heartbeat later at the hospital, is credited with averting a bloodbath that might have taken forty lives.

DOG FETCHES MASTER FROM WHIRLPOOL, DEATH

Over the Thanksgiving holiday in 1975, Zorro the German shepherd gave his master Mark Cooper one more thing to be thankful for. The twenty-six-year-old auto mechanic from Orangevale, California, was hiking in a remote, mountainous area along a steep ravine when he slipped and fell eighty-five feet into a white water river and got trapped in a whirlpool. In his struggle to free himself, he lost consciousness. When he came to, he felt his seventy-five-pound dog trying to drag him up a slippery rock. Zorro lost his grip once and Cooper fell back into the water, but the dog managed to pull him up onto the steep rock. Then Zorro stretched out across Cooper's legs and held him there so he wouldn't fall back in. Cooper was too seriously injured to walk and waited three days for rescuers to find him. Zorro stayed next to him throughout the ordeal, pressing up close to keep him warm. "I wouldn't be alive today if it wasn't for my dog," Cooper said a year later when Zorro was given an award for bravery.

TEEN RESCUES FELLOW COWBOY DRAGGED BY HORSE

Arthur Phillips Jr. and Neal Reed, both sixteen, were on their horses roping sheep on a ranch near Sterling City, Texas, in 1943. After catching a sheep, Neal dismounted and inadvertently stepped in a loop of his lariat that was lying on the ground and still connected to his saddle. Suddenly, his horse became spooked and took off. As the steed broke into a run, the loop tightened around Neal's legs until he was being dragged by the horse. Seeing what happened, Arthur galloped after him. Several times Arthur reached for the reins of Neal's horse, but each time the horse veered off. Meanwhile, Neal was getting battered by being dragged over jagged rocks. Finally, Arthur got his mount within four feet of Neal's horse and, with both steeds at full gallop, he leapt off his horse and onto the neck of Neal's horse. Arthur wrapped his arms around its neck, and held on until his weight pulled the horse's head down enough for it to stop. Neal suffered lacerations and bruises, and Arthur received only minor scratches.

WORKER SAVES CAMPER
FROM VICIOUS BEAR

Landscaper David Michael Calnan, forty-five, was working in a campground near Dawson City, Yukon, in 1999 when a camper rushed over to him, yelling that a bear was attacking a young woman. Calnan dashed to the scene where a black bear was mauling Carrie-Lynne Fair, nineteen. He threw blocks of wood at the bruin to scare it away, but his actions angered the animal, and it charged him twice. Each time, the bear came within a few feet of him before it returned to the injured Fair and dragged her farther away. Calnan picked up a four-foot-long log and repeatedly struck the bear, forcing it to retreat about one hundred feet. Then the bear circled Calnan and Fair a few times. Not until a police officer arrived did the bear run off. Evacuated from the scene, Fair required hospitalization.

For more information: www.carnegiehero.org

"*Superstars strive for approbation; heroes walk alone. Superstars crave consensus; heroes define themselves by the judgment of a future they see it as their task to bring about. Superstars seek success in a technique for eliciting support; heroes pursue success as the outgrowth of inner values.*"

—Henry Kissinger, Secretary of State

STROLLER RESCUES BOY FROM FREAK WAVE

A huge freakish wave roared up on Aberdeen Beach in Scotland in 2004 and washed two boys into the frigid waters. Alastair Farquharson, fifty-four, saw the wave hit the boys and watched as one of them scrambled up a seawall to safety. But the other, twelve-year-old Ryan Smith, was being swept out to sea. Farquharson, who was on the beach promenade only because he had missed a film at a nearby theater, tossed his jacket off, grabbed a life belt, and jumped into the rough seas. When he swam out to Ryan, the boy was unconscious but alive. Farquharson quickly hauled the boy back to land. He was hailed as a hero, but Farquharson said he did nothing extraordinary. "I didn't think about it. I just jumped in and got the boy out. It was no big deal."

TRUCKER BRAVES FLAMES, HAZARDOUS MATERIALS IN RESCUE

"Help, I'm on fire!" came the desperate cry from the trapped driver of a burning tanker truck that had just careened off the highway outside of Jackson, Mississippi, in 2004. Several motorists had stopped, but no one was willing to get near the fiery truck because it had been transporting hazardous materials. When trucker Rick Trask, a former police officer and soldier, arrived on the scene, he didn't hesitate to help. Trask ran to the burning cab and used two hard yanks to free the trapped driver, who was whisked to a burn center. Trask was hailed as a hero, but he brushed it off. "People don't realize what they can do until the time comes," he said. "Instinct kicks in, I guess, but I knew I would have to do whatever I could to help."

SAILOR RESCUES CAT
IN STORMY SEAS

A sailor risked his life to rescue a stubborn cat during a storm on the high seas in 1930. Brutal winds, driving rains, and violent waves were buffeting the South American steamship *El Lobo* as it transported its cargo of fifty thousand barrels of oil to Philadelphia. During the height of the storm, the ship's feline mascot scurried onto the deck. Close behind was Chief Engineer Rudolph Newcastle, determined to get the cat to safety down below. As the two played their game of cat and mouse, a large wave slammed into the tanker, washing both overboard. Somehow, Newcastle snatched the cat out of the foam. Meanwhile, Chief Mate Frank Muldowney tossed out a life preserver. Still clinging to the seafaring feline, Newcastle grabbed hold of the preserver and both were hauled on board.

WITNESS DRAGS ELDERLY MAN FROM SINKING CAR

Andrew Rose watched in stunned amazement as a car zoomed out of control, sped through a pedestrian crosswalk, and slammed into several cars before plunging thirty feet into a lake near Elanora, Australia, in 2004. Wanting to help, Rose, thirty-four, leapt into the water to the sinking car. Inside, an elderly driver was frozen in shock, his eyes glazed. All the windows were closed and the doors were locked. The man was not responding as Rose banged on the window. Finally, Rose managed to push the window down and pull the man out. By the time they reached the shore, the car had vanished under the water. Later at the hospital, doctors determined the man had suffered a seizure. Rose, a carpenter, was on the scene only because he had taken a sick day because of a leg injury. "I was just in the wrong place at the right time," he said.

LAUNDRY LADY GIVES LIFE
SAVINGS TO EDUCATION

"I'm giving it away so that the children won't have to work so hard, like I did," said Oseola McCarty. She was explaining why she gave away her life savings of one hundred fifty thousand dollars that she had accumulated through decades of hard work and thrift as a washerwoman in Hattiesburg, Mississippi. McCarty, an only child, never had an education. She learned she was dying of cancer in 1995 and thought the money she had slowly saved over a lifetime should be spent giving young people opportunities she missed. So she donated her hard-earned fortune to the University of Southern Mississippi for scholarships. News of her generosity turned the humble woman into a celebrity. Hundreds of awards—including the President's Citizen Medal and an honorary degree from Harvard—rolled in. Before her death at age ninety-one in 1999, McCarty had carried the Olympic torch, flipped the switch that dropped the ball in Times Square on New Year's Eve, and shaken hands with the President of the United States. Best of all, her gesture inspired others—following her lead, Ted Turner earmarked a billion dollars for charities.

For more information: www.usm.edu/pr/oolamain.htm

"*Courage is contagious. When a brave man takes a stand, the spines of others are often stiffened.*"

—Billy Graham, evangelist

RESCUE FROM
THE ICE LAGOON

Billie Miller, twenty-two, spotted a struggling figure trapped in the ice in December 1991. Frederick DePerkins, ten, had fallen through a hole in a frozen lagoon in Fontenelle Park in Omaha, Nebraska. Miller carefully walked sixty feet across the ice and extended his jacket to the boy. Frederick clutched it, but when Miller started pulling, the ice below his feet cracked and he fell in. He made his way to Frederick and pushed him out onto the solid ice, allowing him to scramble to shore. Miller tried to move, but found his feet stuck in the mud at the bottom of the lagoon. During his struggle he lost his footing and went under. Luckily, firefighters arrived just in time and pulled him out. They brought him to the hospital, where he was treated for hypothermia and released.

COP GRABS, HOLDS
LIVE GRENADE

Amtrak Police Officer Rodney Chambers and U.S. Capitol Police Officer Michael DeCarlo tried to arrest a disturbed man who had been menacing pedestrians in Washington, D.C., in 2003. The man, later identified as Juann Tubbs, suddenly held up a grenade and pulled the pin. Instead of taking cover, Chambers lunged forward, grabbed the madman's hand, and wrestled the grenade from him. Then Chambers pressed down heavily on the safety catch—known as the spoon—to keep the device from exploding. For fifteen sweaty minutes, Chambers held the spoon tight until the bomb disposal team arrived.

BASSETT HOUND SUMMONS RESCUERS

On an icy day in December 1981, the tractor that Nancy Milestone, seventeen, was operating flipped over, crushing her legs and pelvis. Way out in a field on her family's farm in Mount Horeb, Wisconsin, Nancy screamed for help, but there was no one around except her pet basset hound, Buster. Nancy saw him standing a few feet from her, but figured the dog, whom she had nicknamed Dumbbell, was too stupid to help. Buster surprised her. With no other option, Nancy found a scrap of paper in her jacket pocket and scribbled a plea for help, using her own blood. She attached it to the dog's collar and told him to go home. Buster didn't know this command, but he trotted off in the direction of the farmhouse. A short time later, Nancy's brother rushed out to get her. During her recovery, Nancy learned that Buster had run home and started barking wildly, something that was way out of character for the sleepy little dog. After that, Nancy found a new nickname for her pet. Instead of Dumbbell, she called him Hero.

CLIMBER CARRIES INJURED BUDDY FROM SUMMIT

Mountain hiker Wilbur Page was near the summit of Belknap Mountain in New Hampshire in 1926 when he slipped and broke his ankle. Fortunately, his companion was Victor Sadd, a daring flying ace with the British Flying Corps during World War I. Not one to panic, Sadd calmly set Page's ankle with branches. Then he pulled his injured partner onto his back and walked down the mountain trail, even though Page, at 184 pounds, outweighed him by twenty-four pounds. Once at the base, Sadd got Page into a car and whisked him to a hospital. But it wasn't really necessary. Doctors said that Sadd had so skillfully set the bone on the mountain trail that all they had to do was put a cast around the ankle.

LANDLORD RESCUES
TENANT FROM BLAZE

Jupp Norhausen, fifty-three, rescued a terrified tenant who was hiding in the bathroom after fire broke out in her rented home in Port Orange, Florida, in 2003. Norhausen, an electrical engineer, had to crawl past flames and through rooms filled with acrid black smoke before he found her cowering in the shower. He made her get down on the floor and together they crawled out of the burning house.

"Courage is very important. Like a muscle, it is strengthened by use."

—Ruth Gordon, actress

ROWERS SAVED BY MED STUDENT TEAMMATE

Freakish winds of up to ninety miles per hour in December 2000 overturned two boats containing sixteen members of the Oxford University Lightweight Rowing Club as they trained on the River Ebro at Amposta, Spain. Hugh Wright, a twenty-one-year-old medical student, told his colleagues to hang on to the capsized boats until help arrived. But team member Leo Blockley, twenty-one, lost his grip and was swept away in the strong current. Wright swam after him, looking for him even after Blockley's struggling form vanished under the turbulent water. Wright continued to search until he became so tired he was in danger of drowning himself. Summoning his last reserves of strength, Wright swam more than one hundred yards to shore, where he sounded the alarm. Rescuers saved all the rowers who had stayed with the boats, but sadly, Blockley drowned. For his heroic efforts in trying to save his teammate, Wright was awarded the Royal Humane Society's silver medal.

HERO FROM HISTORY
Clara Barton

Clara Barton was working as a clerk in the Patent Office in Washington, D.C., at the start of the Civil War. As waves of wounded Union soldiers arrived in the city, she realized that the Union had no real plans to deal with its casualties. It took her a year, but she finally persuaded the government to let her travel to the battle-fields with her own medical supplies. At Antietam she braved flying bullets to get supplies to the surgeons and to comfort the wounded and dying. Her tireless efforts at some of the most brutal battles of the Civil War earned her the sobriquet "Angel of the Battlefield." After the war, Barton continued her work, eventually establishing the world's most recognized international relief organization—the American Red Cross.

For more information: www.nps.gov/clba

POOCH RESCUES OWNER
FROM POOL

Kathie Webber and her husband, Chuck, adopted an unwanted chocolate Labrador retriever in the fall of 2001. They named her Carly Simon after Kathie's favorite singer and showered her with love. The dog quickly repaid them with a gift they could never have expected. During an unusual Christmastime cold snap in Ocala, Florida, Kathie was bundled up in layers of clothes, a heavy sweater, coat, and hiking boots while covering her plants. But then she slipped and fell into the deep end of her pool. All the heavy clothing had dragged her to the bottom and she couldn't move. *I can't believe I'm going to drown here in my swimming pool*, she thought. At that moment she heard a howl and a splash. Carly had leapt into the pool. The dog swam in a circle, then lowered her hindquarters so Kathie could grab her tail. The dog then pulled her to the surface. Once on land, Carly covered Kathie's face with kisses. "It was the best Christmas present I ever received," Kathie said.

You can read about more heroic dogs in *Dogmania: Amazing but True Canine Stories* by Allan Zullo and Mara Bovsun (Andrews McMeel Publishing, 2006).

PASSERBY PULLS GIRL
FROM BURNING CAR

In 2002, an accident sent Angela M. Hutsell's car hurtling down an embankment in flames near Ladue, Missouri. Hutsell, nineteen, was unconscious, her body draped out the window on the driver's side, her head inside the car. Kalvin Kabinoff, fifty-three, ran down the embankment and, despite flames that practically engulfed the car, grabbed Hutsell and tried to pull her out through the window. But her seat belt was wrapped around her shoulder, preventing Kabinoff from freeing the unconscious girl, so he had to reach through the fire to remove it. Once he freed her, Kabinoff rolled her on the ground to put out the flames on her body. Hutsell suffered extensive third-degree burns, but she recovered.

STUDENT NABS THIEF WITH PANTS DOWN

When student Gidone Sirick, nineteen, saw a man in jogging clothes fleeing from a jewelry store in Woolwich, South East London, in 2003, he knew the fellow wasn't out for exercise. The man was a jewel thief. So Sirick ran after him and tackled him. In his fierce struggle to break free of the teen's grip, the crook lost his pants and shoes but managed to escape. Sirick turned the garments over to police, who through DNA, discovered the identity of the culprit—Michael Blake, nineteen. Sirick received a commendation from the High Sheriff of Greater London. Blake got three and a half years in prison.

"Courage is the ladder on which all the other virtues mount."

—Clare Boothe Luce, journalist

YOUNG GIRL STEERS SCHOONER THROUGH HURRICANE

When Captain F. W. Patten and most of his crew became deathly ill with beriberi on a sea voyage from Hawaii to Philadelphia in 1905, it came down to one person, his nine-year-old daughter Nellie May, to sail the vessel. Nellie had learned navigation through many hours of standing next to her father while he steered his ship, the seven-masted schooner *Kineo*. With her collie Tam O'Shanter beside her, the iron-willed little girl kept the ship on course, guiding skillfully through the violent winds and monstrous swells of a hurricane that sent many other vessels to the bottom of the sea. Several men died of the disease during the trip. Fortunately Captain Patten recovered in two weeks. "Father said his little skipper—he meant me—could resign with glory now," Nellie May wrote in a diary that was published in a New York newspaper. "He said I had saved all their lives." The ship made port in Philadelphia in November, giving Nellie May the reward she had prayed for throughout her ordeal— Christmas dinner at her grandmother's house in Mount Holly, New Jersey.

PARALYZED BUSINESSMAN HELPS BALTIMORE'S POOR

Allan Tibbels of Baltimore was a successful businessman until his life changed forever after breaking his neck during a basketball game in 1981. Although paralyzed from the chest down, Tibbels decided to devote his life to helping others. He zeroed in on a drug-ridden slum known as Sandtown. First the mostly black residents avoided the peculiar white man in a wheelchair. Then kids became curious. Eventually he earned enough trust to start a church. In 1988, he teamed with Habitat for Humanity and has directed the rehabilitation or building of one hundred sixty new homes. He has also raised $5.5 million for healthcare and learning and job centers. Although he's had to deal with the usual troubles of the inner city—including being robbed at gunpoint—Tibbels has a legion of fans. "His heart is just as big as this world," Glenda Mack told *U.S. News & World Report*. Thanks to Tibbels, Mack, fifty-nine, has become a homeowner for the first time in her life.

MOM CAT RESCUES
KITTENS FROM BLAZE

New York firefighter David Giannelli was battling a blaze in an abandoned garage one icy day in 1996 when he noticed tiny smoke-streaked kittens, first three, then another and another, outside the building. Giannelli couldn't figure out where they were coming from, until he found the mother, a badly burned tortoiseshell with eyes blistered shut. The fearless feline had plunged into the flames to rescue her kittens one by one. Giannelli named her Scarlett, and her heroic deed became an international sensation. The happy ending? Scarlett and four of her five kittens—one died later from a virus—were each adopted by loving families.

RETIREE USES CHAIR TO THWART BANK ROBBERY

In 1999, Louis G. Lalande, a retired steamfitter from Oshawa, Ontario, was doing charity work at a mall when he heard shots coming from a bank across the corridor. He raced to the bank window and saw a robber demanding money from the tellers while firing a starter's pistol at a customer on the floor. Lalande grabbed the nearest weapon he could find—a metal folding chair. Then he stormed into the bank and started swinging. Two good whacks in the head were all it took to stun the gunman and disarm him. Three other men then held the robber down until police came to arrest him.

WATERWORLD STAR TURNS ON WATERWORKS IN BLAZE

On New Year's Eve, 1996, a powerline transformer exploded, causing a fast-growing brush fire in Carpinteria, California. Winds had knocked trees across the roads, blocking firefighters from reaching the blaze, which was raging out of control. Several homes were in the path of the fire. Realizing that something had to be done fast, movie actor Kevin Costner, who lived in the area, grabbed a garden hose and attacked the flames. With the help of a neighbor, Costner finally doused the blaze within an hour. Authorities said that he took an "aw, shucks attitude" toward the whole thing, but the damage might have been extensive had it not been for this real life action hero. Ironically, Costner's most recently released film at the time was *Waterworld*.

"*The courage of life is often a less-dramatic spectacle than the courage of a final moment; but it is no less than a magnificent mixture of triumph and tragedy.*"

—President John F. Kennedy

ABOUT THE AUTHORS

Allan Zullo is the bestselling author of over eighty books, including *Heroes of the Holocaust: True Stories of Rescues by Teens* and *Survivors: True Stories of Children in the Holocaust*. He has been creating and producing bestselling daily calendars since 1989. He has appeared on hundreds of radio and television shows, including *Good Morning America*, the *Today Show*, and the *Late Show with David Letterman*. He lives in Fairview, North Carolina.

For more information about the author, go to www.allanzullo.com.

Mara Bovsun is a magazine editor and freelance journalist who has cowritten several nonfiction books with Allan. She lives in New York City.